ART AND DESIGN ▲●■ EDUCATION SERIES

CRITICAL STUDIES IN ART AND DESIGN EDUCATION

Edited by David Thistlewood

Longman
in association with the
National Society for Education
in Art and Design

Longman Group UK Limited,
Longman House, Burnt Mill, Harlow,
Essex CM20 2JE, England
and Associated Companies throughout the world.

© Longman Group UK Limited 1989

First published 1989
Second impression 1990

Set in 10/12 point Plantin (Linotron 202)
Produced by Longman Group (F.E.) Limited
Printed in Hong Kong

ISBN 0 582 029643

Contents

Contents

Illustrations

Cover: *Improvisation Sintflut*, 1913; Wassily Kandinsky, Städtische Galerie im Lenbachhaus, München, © ADAGP, Paris & DACS, London, 1989.

Introduction

Critical Studies is now an accepted abbreviated term for those parts of the art and design curriculum, in all levels of education, that embrace art history, aesthetic theories, and the social, economic, political, religious and numerous other contexts within which the practice of art and design exists, develops and fulfils its purposes. It is undeniably of increasing importance, and this may be due in part to an understandable tendency, as the twenty-first century approaches, to take stock of past cultural achievements and ensure that they are built into our educational provision. It may also be due to a recent widening of art educationalists' ambitions on behalf of young people. It is not too long ago that these were governed by two general alternatives: either children were being educated as future practitioners of art and design or as consumers of its products. To 'practice' and 'informed consumption' have now been added the concepts 'connoisseurship' and 'visual literacy'.

The former takes consumption far beyond the limited realm of tasteful acquisition. The visual arts, of course, cannot thrive without a demand for their products, but equally they require an informed reception and constructive response on the part of the general population. Conversely, all citizens are entitled to the means of intellectual and emotional access to the full range of creative expressions produced in their culture, not merely those that lend themselves readily to mass marketing. They are also entitled to appreciate the ways in which visual signs and symbols convey meanings to them, often unconsciously or subliminally but always powerfully. One effective means of gaining such appreciation is to examine how symbolism was generated in the past, to analyse historical art production in relation to its attendant social, economic and other contexts, and in the process to gain insights into how today's most potent icons are entering the general consensus.

There is also another, more pragmatic, reason why curricular attention has become focused on *Critical Studies* in Great Britain: this is a direct consequence of our public examination system in the 1960s. Then the introduction of the Certificate of Secondary Education (CSE), beside the longer-established General Certificate of Education (GCE), greatly increased pressures on teachers of all subjects. In art and design, and in the separate subject of art history, the number of examination candidates rose dramatically. Art teachers, faced with the demands of two examination systems and two separate subjects, each requiring fundamentally different teaching methods, inevitably began to demand more resources and increased pupil contact. As these were often unforthcoming, an early casualty in many schools was the provision of art history as a discrete subject.

As a consequence, many teachers felt that an important aspect of their pupils' education in art and design was being neglected for the worst possible—namely, logistic—reasons. It may be, therefore, that a certain residual guilt has led to the present groundswell of support for *Critical*

Studies, including as this does a significant art historical component. That *Critical Studies* is now advocated as an integral part of the art and design curriculum goes a long way to assuaging the concerns of many teachers, but of course it has continually to be borne in mind that teachers are motivated substantially towards teaching that which is assessed.

It is against this background that the Secondary Examinations Council (SEC) has been exploring the possibility of introducing criterion-referenced examinations for the General Certificate of Secondary Education (GCSE). In January 1986 a working party was established to write draft grade criteria for art and design. Its report was published in 1988, and it now seems likely that grade criteria will be introduced in respect of most subjects by 1990. Significantly, the art and design working party opted for a 'three domain' assessment model, one of which is labelled *Contextual and Critical Studies*. Conscious that the introduction of a *compulsory* element of this kind would have considerable resource implications reminiscent of those experienced around twenty years earlier, the working party recommended that this domain should be afforded a 20 per cent weighting, that is, substantially less than if all three were weighted equally.

This area of study then—already a feature of many individual teachers' programmes—will become generally available to pupils and students of all ages. They will become more positively encouraged to express ideas and insights gained in reflection upon their own practical work and that of others. They will be expected to show evidence of some reciprocal effect of their critical perceptions either in their practical work or in supporting studies. They will be encouraged to engage concepts deriving from historical, social, cultural and technological matters that have affected, or now affect, creative production across the entire spectrum of art and design. The necessary teaching provisions cannot fall into place overnight, and therefore one of the questions addressed in this volume of essays is that of curricular materialisation.

This volume's purview is also partly retrospective, and it contains several key contributions to the *Journal of Art and Design Education*, reprinted here because of their importance in the recent history of the development of *Critical Studies*. There is also an equal representation of complementary, previously-unpublished essays, included to ensure a comprehensive coverage. There has been no attempt to present co-ordinated views: several contributors put forward opposing arguments, and occasionally take each other to task. The only uniform feature of this collection is the significant fact that it constitutes a debate that has been fostered in the conferences and house-journal of the **National Society for Education in Art and Design**.

NSEAD.

There are traditional correspondences between British and American art and design education, and it is not merely coincidence that what in Britain is called *Critical Studies* has come to the fore simultaneously in both countries. Elliot Eisner reviews American concerns that first arose over twenty years ago at the prospect of a lop-sided art curriculum, not only biased towards practice but actually favouring uninformed and non-interventionist teaching. Domain models have been elaborated in the resulting research, establishing positive relationships between practical and theoretical disciplines. Eisner puts forward a philosophical justification for a realm-centred approach, argues the fundamental interrelatedness of practical and critical disciplines, and also makes an eloquent plea for including in curriculum models opportunities for spontaneous expression and imaginative response—arguing, in other words, that educational 'structure' is not to be confused with 'regulation'.

In Britain the most significant pioneering achievements in the field of *Critical Studies* have been individual teaching strategies. These developments were presented and debated at many conferences throughout the 1980s, and their underlying principles have thus entered general currency. Prominent has been Rod Taylor's work at Wigan, where the results of involving children in critical dialogues with mature artists and craftspeople have challenged the convention that creative expression is governed by stages of maturity. Less well-known south of the border, but equally effective in Scotland, has been Mike Hildred's successful integration of studies conducted in the classroom, art museum and print workshop. These have encouraged pupils to analyse accepted master paintings in the original and in reproduction, while at the same time studying the commercial processes that make such works the icons of our time. This phenomenon has also been the focus of Andrew Mortimer's work in Cumbria, but the special dimension he has added has been to involve his pupils in the history of the events portrayed in works of art, for example by comparing the 'news' embodied in historic paintings with comparable incidents reported in the media today. Ever since the demise of the Victorian *National Curriculum* there has been a general aversion for encouraging copyist techniques, and a prime concern in visual analytical study is to ensure exhaustive scrutiny of works of art while discouraging thoughtless imitation. Arthur Hughes' concern has been to argue that throughout the history of Western art, making copies and parodies have been regarded as legitimate procedures for understanding and adopting other artists' aesthetic outlooks. His achievements in Birmingham have supported the principle that this ancient form of creative practice may be 'legitimised' by concentrating on the variations that occur between originals and the studies they stimulate.

Such examples of individual experimental teaching as these four, here described in their authors' own accounts, substantially created the consensus that came to be reflected in preparations for a 'core curriculum'. This of course is ironic, given the probability that they would not have had much room to flourish if a rigid curriculum had been effective in their formative stages. This must be accepted as a warning that curricula should contain inbuilt provisions for experimental teaching, which is further to emphasise Eisner's principal argument. It is also echoed by John Bowden, who gives an account of the problems that a teacher may face when his or her pupils or students have no grounding whatsoever in art historical knowledge or critical theories. Here, where conventions cut no ice, there is little option besides unconventional extemporisation. But Bowden argues that even in the initial stages of drawing the uninitiated into discussion of works of art there can be structure and discipline, recognition of which will give purpose to what may otherwise be superficial.

The important skill in conducting critiques, of course, is in guiding discussion without dominating it. Katy Macleod's contribution argues that pupils' imagination and stimulation will certainly be diminished if the flow of teaching information is controlled exclusively by the teacher. Bowden and Macleod are therefore covering similar concerns when they discuss strategies for avoiding outfacing pupils and students by massive expertise. Katy Macleod's recommendation is similar to Rod Taylor's—to encourage children to witness mature art in production, providing them with insiders' familiarity with its content, which they then may discuss relatively easily instead of being overawed by intimidating form. By an extension of her argument it follows that to conduct such teaching in the art gallery promotes familiarity with an otherwise-intimidating institution.

It will be noted that there is a multiple controversy concerning pupil-emulation of mature art, copying, working from reproductions, and studying works which, because of their cultural 'advancement', may be considered inappropriate for children's engagement. Brandon Taylor contributes to this latter argument, maintaining that certain twentieth century idioms are inaccessible to children who may nevertheless appear to understand them by simply copying their superficial appearances. He argues for caution in the matter of supplying images for pupil use, suggesting that study should be confined to images conforming to society's majority preference for naturalistic representation. He is therefore on the side of control that Macleod is at pains to oppose. He is also opposed, by Maureen Price, specifically on the question of whether children may comprehend abstraction. To her they have a right of access to this, an idiom of immense contemporary significance, and the question of its difficulty is therefore irrelevant—it is a teaching responsibility to make it comprehensible. In recognition of this Tony Dyson suggests ways in which art history may be structured for teaching pupils of varying ability and sense of involvement in art production. He puts forward a comparative model featuring the study of sets of images of thematic content but contrasting form. This puts the emphasis on interrogation of meaning, rather than appearance, supporting discussion at many different levels of appreciation.

Thematic structuring of a different kind is the concern of Tony Collins. Whereas Dyson sorts by subject-matter Collins organises the material of art history according to 'problematics'. The aesthetic tasks that artists set themselves, and the recurrence of these throughout history, are the phenomena that connect historical study directly to the current efforts of students working in the art school studio. For him the most positive way for art history to be taught is by calling up relevant precedents tactically, rather than by offering a conventional course in which the great movements must be taken in prescribed order. As Rosalind Billingham implies, there is a fundamental opposition of interests here between the historian's and the practitioner's, because while the former's discipline is inclusive the latter's tends exclusively to focus on matters of special significance. Whereas Collins relies on reacting to his students' practical initiatives, drawing on precedents to shore up confidence in problematics that have already been perceived, however indistinctly, Billingham maintains the priority of historical initiatives, themselves giving rise to practical responses.

Finally in this volume John Swift addresses a subject—namely a form of in-service *Critical Studies* for teachers—that in a sense has first priority, in the way that it may nurture the kind of experimental attitudes to curricular research that are obvious in the work of his fellow contributors. He argues that throughout the history of devolved curricula a great many innovators have practised models of teaching that have not diminished in value merely through age. Because of the individual nature of curriculum planning, however, most of these have been discontinued with the cessation of their authors' professional involvement. Those that are represented in our growing number of *Art and Design Education Archives*, however, may be retrieved for re-evaluation. He offers examples of how these relatively unfamiliar institutions may be utilised, and it is interesting that he recommends controlled emulation of other teachers' strategies, as a means of gaining insights into essential problems that are often not apparent in the day-to-day routine. This is precisely the argument in favour of critical study of works of art: it provides contact with an essence by means of close familiarity with exemplars.

I should like to thank all these authors for their contributions to a wide ranging analysis of the rationales, disciplines, purposes and effective means of *Critical Studies* in art and design education. It has been my pleasant task to co-ordinate them and, in the opening chapter, to present arguments for the social relevance of this collective identification. In the process I take a ride on my own hobby horse, which is to point out that the art museum is not an innocuous, neutral institution, but rather one whose almost overpowering cultural symbolism may only be negotiated with the aid of informed and sensitive teaching, and a form of public participation that circumvents ingrained conventions.

DAVID THISTLEWOOD

Chapter One

DAVID THISTLEWOOD Critical Studies, the Museum of Contemporary Art and Social Relevance

Critical Studies is a collective term embracing a multitude of objectives and methods. Somewhere within its purview is old-fashioned 'art appreciation', conveying the principle that children should become familiar with the great themes of painting and sculpture—religious devotion, landscape, the figure, portraiture, still-life, and so forth—as vital aspects of their cultural heritage. This has a very long pedigree, stemming in Britain from at least the seventeenth century, when it was considered essential for all cultured persons to know of civilisation's birth in Ancient Greece and its rebirth in the city states of medieval Italy. *Critical Studies* also encompasses the more academically-laden 'art history', providing the means of ordering successions of artists, innovations and movements throughout the centuries. As a substance for popular dissemination this has a much shorter pedigree. In the 1930s it was the preserve of Professors of Fine Art and committed amateurs, and even as recently as the 1960s, when it became a prescribed subject in British colleges of art, there were far too few trained art historians to share around. 'Complementary studies' was introduced as an extender and enricher of 'art history', with the effect that art students came to see their discipline through the eyes of sociologists, environmentalists and scientists, as well as historians. The resulting hybrid was the forerunner of modern *Critical Studies*, spreading throughout higher education in art and entering secondary schools a generation later.

However, despite the growth of *Critical Studies*, there is little consensus as to its academic nucleus. Some teachers believe its purpose is to make sure that works of art, which otherwise might only be glanced at, are scrutinised as thoroughly as possible. Some say it is only relevant if it ultimately informs practice, and to them its curricular value resides in the ways it brings to their pupils experiences of new techniques or unsuspected subject-matter. Others are committed to the converse of this, arguing that its purpose is to approach a better understanding of the wider world, by seeing this world as artists have seen it. This approach assumes different cultural dimensions when, for example, 'exotic' or 'popular' art replace mainstream Western art at the focus of enquiry. Other teachers maintain that it is chiefly significant for bringing home to pupils the great socio-economic potency of art. And others again argue that it is a means of parading evidence of conventional history—nations, wars, dynasties and revolutions—all of which have left traces embedded in works of art.

It becomes clear, then, why *Critical Studies* is a plural term: it is no single subject with clear-cut aims. It is therefore appropriate to look for definitions, or at least some sense of general purpose and justification underlying this extensive category of art education. In lexical terms it must be 'critical', and by common acceptance this relates to 'criticism' rather than 'crisis' (although a secondary meaning, as in 'critical mass', may be significant for the sense it imparts of an essential 'chain reaction'). It must also involve 'study'—the study of works of art as things in themselves, or of the processes that produce these artefacts, or of their relationships with the world of circumstances in which they are created. For a loose but workable definition it may be said that *Critical Studies* is the sphere of art education that brings works of art into informed, rather than casual, perception by analysing their aesthetic presence, their formative processes, their spiritual, social, economic, and political causes, and their cultural effects. This may seem vague but it nevertheless promotes two certainties: whatever *Critical Studies* may be in all its necessary forms, it requires positive teaching; and because artefacts which are deemed to be works of art stem from realms of extraordinary achievement, this necessary teaching often features the communication of rare and sophisticated concepts.

The danger is of course that a simple equation will be made between *looking at* works of art, however thoroughly, and *appreciating* them. If works of art are merely subjected to naïve analysis they may become thoroughly known as combinations of form, colour, texture and mass, but little will be understood about the religious, historical, social, political, economic, and other motives which may have given rise to them. A van Gogh painting of *Potato Eaters* will be seen as a harmless rendering of a homespun theme, and not as the biting, socio-political commentary on hard toil and marginal existence it undoubtedly was. Picasso's *Guernica* may be thought a curious mixture of ancient and modern symbolism: it may be possible to empathise with its obvious rage, but this will be an abstract identification until its contexts of Spanish Civil War and blitzkrieg are elaborated.

On the other hand, if such contexts are entered into obsessively there is the corresponding danger that works of art may be considered merely the by-products of unaesthetic processes. How often is it said that twentieth century art is a manifestation of our increasing knowledge of human psychology, ignoring the truth that it is one of the principal instruments by which this knowledge has been gained? Conventional art historians are partly to blame here because they have tended to concentrate upon easily communicated incidents. We have been told relatively little about Turner's techniques of grounding, underpainting, glazing, and varnishing (which identify him as meticulous perfectionist), but informed excessively about his delirium for light (which presents him as automatist). We know a great deal about Blake's iconography and religious fervour, but a systematic explanation of his watercolour luminosity has received low priority.

Few art historians are practitioners, and so it is perhaps not surprising that the aesthetic means of art should have had relatively little attention. This cannot be said of members of the museums service, however,

1   VINCENT VAN GOGH   *The Potato Eaters*, 1885, oil on canvas 32·25 × 44·9″; Stedelijk Museum Amsterdam. (photo: Bridgeman Art Library)

2   PABLO PICASSO *Guernica*, 1937; oil on canvas 138 × 308″; Museo del Prado, Madrid, © DACS, 1989.

because their responsibilities to conservation oblige them to understand their charges minutely as physical structures. But they communicate this understanding to one another in their specialist journals, and it hardly

3

ever percolates into spheres of art production and art education. Britain has a very sparse history of popular education in art, involving the handling of exhibits or art-making in their presence, *instigated by museums* where, after all, its best exemplars are expected to be found. And in our institutions that *are* committed to art education—our schools, colleges, polytechnics and universities—any close acquaintance with paintings and sculptures is invariably conducted through the medium of photography.

Our art museums are concerned to be popular, and measure this property by means of attendance totals; but they trade principally in the act of witness, and appear indifferent as to whether this is informed or uninformed. This results in a very strange phenomenon, a kind of inverted reality, according to which the art-objects themselves seem to be 'larger than life', and therefore unreal, versions of works which, perhaps because they have been reproduced in a book or screened in a lecture, are much more real in these forms, sustained as they are by information. A substantial majority of that portion of our population which is interested in art will perceive an hierarchy of reality which has been determined by the literature of art, by television or by formal education, but in any case outside the museum *where the real objects reside*. In this scale of values the photographed image, supported with contextual explanation about precedents, intentions, technique, and credibility-enhancing incident, will rank relatively high. The original work of art, on the other hand, perhaps having colours which have not photographed well, or contours which have flattened in the print or under television lighting, will seem familiar but with distinctly unfamiliar aspects, and will rank low. Unfamiliarity will be likely to be both visual and conceptual, for any efforts the museum may make towards explanation (perhaps conveyed by means of cataloguing and labelling) will have assumed insidious purposes geared much more to provenance than promulgation. And original works which have escaped publication, because they are either minor examples of older art or examples of the very new, will remain largely unreal until 'realised' through education.

There are essentially two ways of encouraging public participation in the museum of art, but whichever is chosen there is no avoiding such educational responsibilities. The museum must either popularise its offerings and draw people in, or it must take its exhibitions into public places. It may be reasoned that working on location is an acceptable temporary expedient if it leads ultimately to persuading people to cross the museum's own threshold. But this does not automatically follow. It was recognised by government in the Second World War, and afterwards during the period of reconstruction, that participation in the arts encourages social identification and cohesion, and substantial resources were expended on taking arts experiences into factories and workshops, schools and community halls throughout the country. However, when support was gradually withdrawn there was no noticeable shift towards museum attendance: participation dwindled as educational programmes diminished. There will probably always be a minority who will engage in the arts autonomously, but public participation on a wider scale requires continuous educational nurturing.

This ought to require museums of art to have whole-time and positive (rather than occasional and passive) educational purposes, but some of their most powerful conventions weigh against this. The commissioners of our first specially-designed public art museum, the Dulwich Picture Gallery, emphasised its exclusive and unworldly nature by incorporating into it, in a prominent position by its entrance, the mausoleum of its patrons. And if it required an effort of will, in spite of the building's magnificence, to enter a *tomb* of art, it was only slightly less traumatic to visit the original British Museum in Montague House, for which admission tickets had to be sought (adequate references having been provided) at least two weeks in advance of a rapid, highly-regimented tour of its contents. Such prototypes as these have in effect been stereotypes. The result has been a legacy of powerful, impressive but not very welcoming buildings, together with a tendency to ensure that whatever educational functions they have fulfilled have been passive.

This begs questions concerning the symbolic meaning which is attached to art museums themselves as works of art, and it becomes apparent that though they have fused a vast range of cultural values they have tended to assimilate these to a dominant architecture of Classicism, reinforcing assumptions that their constituency is art that has stood the test of time. This is why naturalistic art is preferred in our culture at large: our art museums themselves belong in its ambience and cannot help proclaiming its values. Charged with preserving and honouring the great art of the past, and with recognising comparative achievements in the present, they are essentially conservative. Even 'revolutionary' art, when admitted to their collections, becomes bound to the cultural conventions it once utterly rejected, and is thus conservatised.

Critical Studies enters a minefield here because—especially in view of the apparent innocuousness of the popular class visit—it is important to realise the enormous potency of art museums as cultural condensers. Various influences from throughout the world have become synthesised in them, to the extent that today's museum of art, considered as a general type, embodies such principles as an egalitarian pride legated by the earliest European republics, a Russian belief that art is a tribute not to individuals but to peoples, an American respect for excellence, a Japanese belief in the regenerative value of spiritual contemplation, a German approach to systematic interpretation, a British concept of accessibility, and a universal respect for the value of cultural preservation. Put another way, it is a mixture of palace, popular monument, academy, temple, laboratory, public domain and treasure house. In this sense it is not an institution to which schoolchildren (or any other citizens) should be introduced casually or ignorantly, for its massive cultural assumptions will be impossible for them to disregard. Introductions to the art museum, and especially to its contents, must be guided, that is, accompanied by teaching. The necessary tuition, of course, is that which comes under the general heading *Critical Studies*: what is emphatically not required in primary and secondary education is the passive reception of art history's conventional wisdoms.

This is especially true if we accept children's rights of access to their contemporary creativity. Convention deals with contemporary art by attaching it to the past, anchoring it to long-established meaning and thus distorting its significance here and now. Contemporary art is presented as a series of logical outcomes of past styles, and museums are organised as galleries of progressive change. But this is to sanitise contemporary art, explaining it by reference only to older art rather than the current aesthetic, material, theoretical, religious, historical, social, political, economic, and other phenomena which have shaped it. According to accepted practice, attaching contemporary art to the past is the task of the art historian, one of whose other responsibilities is to breathe life into deflated subject-matter. There would be no need to breathe life into contemporary art if its vitality were not systematically extinguished in order to make it presentable.

We have an extremely perverse chain of events. Contemporary art is *detached* from the real circumstances which gave rise to it, and then *attached* to the art of earlier generations, which may have arisen from fundamentally different circumstances. These connections become fixed as crude categorisations, in the face of which art historians must labour to discover and promulgate original meaning. Society at large then finds this meaning in books or on television, and associates it with art's images or objects as reproductions. The distillation of meaning would occur so much more spontaneously, and from the outset be attached to originals, if historians, critics and theorists were not principally motivated towards immediate verbal interpretation.

Contemporary art will lend itself to verbal explanation eventually (it seems always to have done so in the past), but its earliest verbal attachments will be speculative, tentative, often inaccurate, and unconvincing. There is a recognised delay before contemporary art becomes intelligible to the general public: the Monets which were indecipherable in their day are now on every sitting-room wall. What cannot be conveyed in words, however, may be apprehended in practical dialogue, and the most productive way of identifying with contemporary art is to effect forms of critical practice featuring emulation, deconstruction, and creative response. To the catalogue of embodiments in the museum of today, from palace to laboratory, therefore, must be added a Dutch conception—the 'creativity centre'. It is in this sense that our museums of art, particularly our museums of contemporary art, must become centres of practice for the community at large.

Now this begins to suggest the desirability of having different kinds of teaching museum, one general type perhaps geared to art that is distinctly of the past, husbanding conventions, and another committed to engaging the new. *Critical Studies* would of course trade in both, but whereas the former market-place would be structured and orderly, the latter would be chaotic, for the most significant aesthetic phenomenon of the twentieth century has been the disunity of unco-ordinated transformation. Beginning with the work of the Pre-Raphaelite Brotherhood, the first sustained attempt in Britain to shake off classical conventions, an unprecedented range of alternative perceptual values has been explored. The ramifications of this are suggested by the fact that

6

Impressionism, Cubism, Vorticism, Social Realism, Surrealism, Constructivism, Abstract Expressionism, Superrealism, Organicism, Neo-Romanticism, Pop Art and Op Art, New Figuration, Post-Painterly Abstraction, Body, Land and Installation Art, Conceptualism and Minimalism have represented radically different states of consciousness, as opposed to Naturalism, the principal state embodied in the whole of the rest of post-Renaissance art.

It is understatement to say that within a hundred years there has been a vast enlargement of the range of possible and acceptable creativity we call 'art', and that the educational role of the art museum has diminished as this has expanded. Of course, it is simplistic to maintain that before the modern period art had well-understood, entrenched purposes; but before modernism there were few proclaimed attempts—in ways which have become common in the twentieth century—to explore aesthetic concepts so radical that they would initiate far-reaching changes of thought and conduct. Realistic representation and the deployment of widely-understood symbols held primacy for around five hundred years. It is true that throughout much of this period most works of art were intended for private, or relatively-localised, appreciation; but the essentially 'open' nature of their form and content ensured that they would be intelligible to all who saw them.

It is equally simplistic to describe twentieth century avant-garde art as obscure, but, in spite of artists' professions to be addressing people in the mass, the tendency to originate creative themes in private research (because we do not have public studios and workshops, such as the museums ought to provide) *has* resulted in idioms and symbols which remain 'closed' to general appreciation for considerable periods. This is an unproductive interval, preventing rapport between those who are compelled to express particular visual and plastic concepts and those who might reasonably be expected to be receptive to their expressions.

We may consider any one of the well-known 'isms' at random—Vorticism, say—and be confident that though it may be widely recognized now, through its gradual percolation into mass consciousness, Lewis, Bomberg, Etchells, Roberts, Nevinson and their associates would have benefited from a substantial response of sympathisers, critics, imitators and collaborators before 1920, when, while their *concepts* were ignored, their work was being salted away as investment. In the case of Lewis there was a thirty year delay before his work was interpreted to the general public (in the Tate Gallery's retrospective exhibition of 1952). A cynic may perhaps be forgiven for doubting whether Vorticism would ever have emerged from the archives (in the process becoming, for the first time, a potential subject for analytical teaching) without the art historian's force of external persuasion (which would have been unnecessary if the idiom's values had been taught from their outset).

Once in train, however, revived awareness of Vorticism gradually intensified and led to major re-evaluation in 1974, in a definitive exhibition at the Hayward Gallery, a building whose mid-twentieth century 'brutalism' dwarfed and distorted the small-scale, hard, smart and sharply angular aesthetic of its temporary contents. It may be speculated that if our major museums had systematically presented their holdings in Vorticism in the most sympathetic way (instead of confining them to storage), educating in their values and also responding to changes in informed public perception, there would have existed in the 1970s an authentic Vorticist environment, precluding the need to exhibit them in an alien setting. This is to maintain that at least some museums—especially those that are styled museums of *contemporary* art—should be repositories of living art, rather than art which has subsided into sedimentary history.

This means more than merely opening museums to new art, for it is contradictory to profess to interpret new creative concepts if these are seen to have been ineffectual in relation to the museum's own fabric and organisation. For the museum can never be, as many suppose it is, an aesthetically neutral environment. Its form is bound to embody significance, if only by default, and the commonest 'default' significance, of course, is that engendered by the great eighteenth and nineteenth century preoccupation with Classical architecture and its attendant naturalism in painting and sculpture. This harks to a time when the only works of art considered 'authentic' were ancient marbles and their 'true' descendants of the High Renaissance. These were finite in number and were to be revered, requiring them to be housed in appropriately designed settings which would fit them for the rest of time.

It would be preposterous to maintain that art education today should be geared to such principles, but this is the 'default' significance which remains operative until countered by substantial *Critical Studies* teaching. Yet even when this is most effective it still has to contend with the fact that the intended setting for most accomplished art—the art museum—is invariably permeated with a contrived architectural Classicism (contrived in the sense that it brings a Greek and Roman language of form to a building type which did not exist in the ancient world). And when this constitutes the surroundings of works which are not remotely Classical in origin, or which are principally formless or informal as compared with its powerful formality, the result is dilution which is often total. How may monumentality be expressed in filaments or membranes when this property is caricatured in the massive presence of surrounding architecture? How may rough-edged industrial materials sit easily beside the most luxurious finishes and finely-detailed surfaces? They cannot without sacrificing their potential significance, for even the debased Classicism of a seedy museum interior invokes the full authority of Europe's most enduring symbols of civilization. One of the purposes of *Critical Studies* is to educate in these symbols: another, co-equally, is to proffer the alternatives which are originating in contemporary art. The former requires the co-operation of art museums: the latter demands the collaboration of museologists, educationists, and contemporary art's practitioners to recreate the museum in a form encouraging participation.

What will this new form take? This cannot be preconceived, but it seems likely that a movement towards it will be led by educationists (teachers of *Critical Studies* in schools and also in museums), and not merely served by them. Indeed the present *Critical Studies* momentum may have an obvious consequence in prompting museums of contemporary art to be inherently *critical* themselves. Of course, they are already implicitly critical in the ways in which they make deliberate, well-reasoned selections from currently-available works of art, and gradually add to and subtract from these in the search for more complete statements of the values their collections represent. But this should not be the limit of their critical activities. They should subject their collections to *explicit*, systematic re-evaluation by engaging the public in continual critical dialogue.

There are differences of interest here. Art museums generally concur with an existing logic, but their users, from committed scholars to casual visitors, come to find unique significance. Art museums organise their holdings to fit established rationales. They do not find histories expressed in the works they care for, but they care most reverently for (and seek hardest to acquire) works which best illustrate accepted histories. In concurring with, and reinforcing, conventions they discourage those who attend museums from constructing their own rationales. This is a plea, not for disorganised presentation, but for changing presentations in recognition of differently-perceived significance. This would require some admission that aesthetic judgements are tentative, and derive as much from outside influences as from the museum's own authority. It would also require greater attention to the fact that art has substantial social, as well as individual, significance: the art museum of the future is likely to be an *interactive* organism.

Together with equivalent disciplines such as music, literature and science, art plays a major role in the formation of conceptual definitions, giving them shape, tangibility and memorable potency. This is a principal way in which people orientate themselves in relation to past, present and future, and symbolise their emotions and beliefs by fixing upon concrete forms. It is a process rooted in individuation—in the creation of images by individual artists. But as these images are discovered by others and are gradually disseminated throughout widening circles of appreciation, they gain general currency and become agents of group identification. In this way Whistler's *Arrangement in Grey and Black No. 1* has come to symbolise many of our emotions towards elderly motherhood, and Yeames's *And When Did You Last See Your Father?* has become one of the relatively few images by which an event singularly lacking in palpable reality today, the English Civil War, is suddenly brought within range of our feelings. Occasionally such potency may transcend disciplinary boundaries, as for example when Picasso's painting, Stravinsky's music, Joyce's literature and Einstein's scientific philosophy coincided to express fragmentary and crystalline human experience around the First World War. The works of these individuals are more than mutual analogies: they are identical or near-identical concepts embodied in different forms. Later Jackson Pollock's Action Painting symbolised contemporary psychological concepts of the shallow unconscious so effectively that even today it is inseparably associated with Freud.

Thus a very few images eventually assume national or even inter-

3   JAMES MCNEILL WHISTLER
Arrangement in Grey and Black No. 1, 1872, oil on canvas 56·75 × 64"; Louvre, Paris. (photo: Reunion des Musées Nationaux, Paris)

national significance, but for every one of these there are countless that are meaningful to special interest groups, and to smaller and smaller communities of individuals, in effect creating conceptual bonds between individuals and communities as recognition of these images grows. Of course this process may go too far and images become so widely disseminated that they become clichés—witness Leonardo's *Mona Lisa* and Munch's *The Scream*. However, if *Critical Studies* has a prior function in dissemination it also has a subsequent responsibility towards revitalisation, and one service it ought usefully to perform would be to ensure that popular images are actually observed as keenly as the less-familiar.

A new and forward-looking museum policy would therefore recognise that the general public have an interest in determining aesthetic significance that is as pressing, in its own way, as the interests of art historians. There is another dimension to this concept, however, which requires sensitivity towards the probability that art is the product not only of

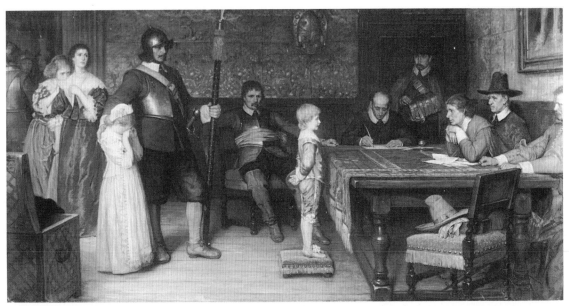

4   WILLIAM FREDERICK YEAMES *And When Did You Last See Your Father?*, 1878, oil on canvas 51·5 × 99″; Walker Art Gallery, Liverpool.

individual, but also of collective, creativity. In this sense the museum must of course draw attention to the uniqueness of artists' perceptions, but it should also celebrate the cultural processes that give rise to artists themselves and thus significantly shape their art. Consider the analogies of poetic and everyday language. Poetry, like much of the visual arts, is manifested in individual acts of creativity, for although it has the power to transmit the most profound ideas and meanings (as in Shakespearian drama) it is unusable as an everyday medium of communication. It is an extraordinary, particular and intense form of contact, in which recipients expect to be attuned to heightened perception and prime their senses accordingly. Poetry cannot function for the unreceptive.

In contrast, prose and language are media of general communication, and cater more or less efficiently to a great range of receptivity, from the attentive to the unattentive. So if art and poetry are considered comparable as individual modes of creativity, it seems reasonable to assume that there is some generalising of visual and formal concepts, functioning in the world at large, that relates to art in the same way that prose and language relate to poetry. If this is put in a slightly different and perhaps more acceptable way, it may be suggested that if poetry is regarded as a form of immediate communication, in which perception and expression are spontaneously fused, then its word-associations (poets rarely invent new words) enter general language as people gradually become accustomed to them, and modify them to fit increasing varieties of purpose.

The socialisation of art may be said to be an exact parallel of this, suggesting at once why museums of contemporary art are of vital necessity—they recognise and give first expression to immediate percipience—and why *Critical Studies* is indispensable to the fulfilment of their paramount purpose. It bridges (or should bridge) the symbolism

11

of avant-garde creativity and popular currency, taking part in the moulding process by which 'unique' concepts become 'multipurpose' concepts, and constantly relating these generalisations back to their roots in acts of original invention. It first triggers the development of awareness of avant-garde art for a general audience, and then continuously re-stimulates this process.

This ought to happen in several distinct ways. It already does function at the level of origination in British art, thanks to the now-established, singular requirement for art students to cultivate critical attitudes towards their own production. It does not yet function at the point of exposition because there is no firm tradition obliging museums to comment on the news they break, beyond establishing its authenticity and provenance. Catalogues expound virtues but never transgressions, and invariably manage to exude airs of faultlessness around their subjects. Neither does it yet function adequately at the level of disseminating, reshaping and adapting visual and formal concepts as they are modified for general usage. This is the principal sphere of *Critical Studies*, although it also has a part to play in countering the convention of the 'homage' exhibition. One way, for example, in which this would be effective would be for *Critical Studies* to be regarded as a normal museum provision, and a standard aspect of every exhibition.

Most of the benefits of all of this must reside in the realm of potential until they are actually put into effect experimentally, but one result at least may be anticipated. The propagation of art is a process which *does* take place, irrespective of whether it is noticed by the general public. Much of the symbolism that was once attached uniquely to avant-garde movements such as Cubism and Constructivism is now evident in architectural design. The same is true of Surrealism, Op Art, and other once-contemporary idioms, in street advertising and store display. It may be safe to assume that all the concerns of avant-garde art will eventually become the properties of architecture, graphic design and even fashion design, because the practitioners of these disciplines look to avant-garde invention for insights into their own aesthetic preoccupations. In this way, and at some delay, highly original visual and formal concepts enter the public environment. The symbolisms of other times and cultures, too, become annexed because designers continually search for novel, as well as new, signification.

Architects and graphic designers are the agents of transmission, but of course they have no remits to educate in the symbols they transmit. So the enormous visual and formal variety within our stock of buildings is an object of educational neglect and public indifference. *Critical Studies* has an obvious role here, though it must concern itself with more than mere observation. It must promote thorough understanding of symbolic origination by tracing the roots of common visual and formal concepts to their origins in movements and works of art. If it is asked why this should be necessary when it has not been considered worth-while before, it should be pointed out that in Britain 'environmental quality' has usually come a poor second to commercial exploitation. However, 'environmental quality' is now of paramount importance, but the public has few general standards of discernment. A critical understanding of how visual and formal concepts come into being in art—of how they are grasped, sketched out, refined, redrawn, distorted, discarded, regained, reshaped, justified and criticised in their formative processes—would give insights into relevant criteria. Moreover, the public's identification with these processes *as practitioners* (and therefore as investors) would ultimately result in enhanced environmental percipience and respect. This is the case that all those involved in *Critical Studies* should be arguing, for nothing is more likely to prompt advancement on political agendas, and bring art and our art museums from the periphery to the focus of social relevance.

Acknowledgements

I should like to thank the *Royal Society of Arts W J Parker Trust* for providing opportunities for me to review the educational provisions of a number of European and American art museums. I should also like to acknowledge the importance to me of the museum educational philosophy of Jean Leering, formerly Director of the Van Abbe Museum, Eindhoven: his ideas are especially evident in my discussion of the modern art museum's self-critical responsibilities, the poetic analogy, the potentially harmful effect of the 'homage' exhibition, and the necessary focus of *Critical Studies* on environmental issues.

Chapter Two

ELLIOT EISNER Structure and Magic in Discipline-Based Art Education

About a quarter of a century ago, in the aftermath of Russia's stunning achievement in space, the reassessment of American education became an important national priority. This reassessment concluded that America's schools were in need of a solid programme of studies to replace what was regarded as an overly loose curriculum, largely out of touch with the newest and most exciting intellectual achievements in the major disciplines. The result of these concerns was the creation of a variety of new curricula, primarily in the sciences, developed mainly by university academics and intended to bring rigour and theoretical coherence to what students studied in secondary schools.

Art educators were not immune to the climate of the period. Those of us who were around at the time were also motivated to re-examine our field to see if we too could bring more substance and structure to what we were teaching and, perhaps more important, to re-examine our thinking about what we ought to be teaching. The products of our efforts were conveyed in articles such as Manuel Barkan's 'Transition in Art Education' [1]; Vincent Lanier's 'Schizmogenesis in Art Education' [2]; and my own article 'Curriculum Making for the Wee Folk: Stanford University's Kettering Project' [3]. What these articles had in common was the degree to which they made problematic, long-held beliefs about the function of art in the child's education and in the ways that art should be taught. We questioned the view that the development of the child's general creativity was *the* major aim for art education. We questioned the view that working with art materials was the sole vehicle for teaching art in the schools. We questioned the view that the major function of the teacher was to provide materials and reassurance, but seldom instruction. In short, we advanced the idea that the arts have something special to offer to the child, something indigenous to art. We argued that artistic learning included more than being able to use art materials, and we conceptualised a role for the teacher that was far more active and demanding than simply being a provider of art materials and emotional support.

The ideas we advanced from platforms and journals became lively intellectual fare for those of us who work in universities. We read our colleagues' work. We debated their ideas at conferences and conventions. We asked our students to read what we published. Alas our well-intentioned—and I think basically sound—ideas about the teaching of art did not have any major impact on the schools, the very places where our ideas should have counted the most. The reasons for our weak effects on practice are numerous, but one of the most significant is that, unlike science education, our field had very little support from either private foundations or public agencies to help us operationalise within curricula what we had conceptualised in our universities. In addition, at that time, publishers were reluctant to invest their resources in materials that were clearly going to be more expensive than textbooks and required instructional devices they were unaccustomed to producing, especially when the market, compared to the language arts, mathematics, or the social studies, was so small. Ideas, even good ideas, without tenacious support, both financial and moral, have a hard time surviving when they belong to a field that has historically been regarded as educationally marginal.

I believe times have changed. America has almost completed its preoccupation with 'back to the basics'. People are increasingly realising that a decent education for their children requires more than the simple skills of learning to read, write and compute. As efforts at curriculum reform, *circa* 1987, have fallen into place, the fine arts are gradually being given a legitimate place in our schools. In 1979 only one state required a course in the arts as a condition for high school graduation. At present twenty states do [4], and universities and colleges are now giving academic credit for work in the fine arts at the high school level. For example, my own institution, Stanford University, will now consider portfolios, slides, cassettes, video tapes, compositions, and other evidence of artistic accomplishment from students seeking admission. We are making progress, although it would be Pollyannaish for me to suggest that the distance we have yet to travel is short.

However, as the result of concerted action over the past few years, new conceptions of the philosophical worth and practical organisation of art teaching have grown in acceptance, identified under the general title *discipline-based art education*, with which I myself am in full accord [5]. These ideas are not without their critics, and thoughtful critics at that. In view of this, I would like to identify the relevant issues as I see them, I hope allay some fears, to discuss the meaning of 'structure' in discipline-based art education programmes, and finally to remind readers of what the arts are about in schools.

Art educators have historically prided themselves that art is one of the very few subjects in the school's curriculum that gives the child opportunities to draw upon his emotions as a source of content that allows his imagination to take wings. It is art that provides the temporary escape from the rule-governed features of an overly verbal and numerical curriculum. And it is art where the child is encouraged to confer his personal vision and his signature upon his work. Schools are dominated by curricular tasks that are teacher-directed and that too often have one correct solution to every problem, one right answer to every question. What children desperately need is relief from the relentlessness of rule-governed algorithms. What they need is the space, the place and, most of all, the permission to follow the beat of their own drummer, to take risks and, at times, to fail. What children need is *lebensraum*—room for living. The arts must not become the lifeless, mechanistic and dry academic study that has befallen so much of what we teach at all levels of education.

Some in the field today are concerned that in our desire to provide structure in our art programmes and to secure academic legitimacy, the magic of art will be lost. In the end, they fear, we might win the battle but surely lose the war. One writer, concerned about the potentially technocratic character of discipline-based art education comments:

> Charges of technocratic rationality, however, remain perhaps the most difficult issue concerning discipline-based art education—an issue that will not be settled by curriculum committees identifying substantive art content or by the ordering of art slides, reproductions, and books. When art is promoted as providing unique educational benefits, it can be easily dismissed as a frill. When art is presented as structured subject matter, it gains educational legitimacy, but is concomitantly open to charges of reductionism [6].

Another writer asks:

> Do we agree that programs [from Kindergarten to Grade 12] will need to be developed that teach content from four disciplines: art history, art production, art criticism, and aesthetics? Do we agree that art programs should employ the same standards maintained in other academic subjects: written, sequential curriculum; student assessment; and adequate instructional time? [This position has been taken by some] . . . but there are alternative views that offer different translations of a discipline-based approach [7].

These concerns are of course, not new. They reflect two classical tensions in the history of American education. In one view, the starting point for educational decision-making is the child, his needs, his interests, his unique development. The other view begins with the subject-matter to be learned, its values, its structure, its unique features. The tension between these views is also reflected in an emphasis on selecting curriculum content that has immediate personal relevance for the child, as contrasted with a view that considers the discipline as autonomous and whose intellectual integrity has to be protected. The child-centred view emphasises the importance of cultivating personal idiosyncrasy; the subject-centred view tends to have a much higher regard for order and specificity. The latter defines effective education as leading to the successive approximation of a predefined end state. The former sees education as a journey of unfolding and surprising developments that teachers should encourage and exploit. One writer describes these views as follows:

> The fundamental opposition of child and curriculum set up by these two modes of doctrine can be duplicated in a series of other terms. 'Discipline' is the watchword of those who magnify the course of study; 'interest' that of those who blazon 'The Child' upon their banner. The standpoint of the former is logical; that of the latter psychological. The first emphasizes the necessity of adequate training and scholarship on the part of the teacher; the latter that of need of sympathy with the child, and knowledge of his natural instincts. 'Guidance and control' are the catchwords of one school; 'freedom and initiative' of the other. Law is asserted here; spontaneity proclaimed there [8].

The author of the statement above is John Dewey, the date 1902, the book *The Child and the Curriculum*. Thirty-six years later Dewey felt compelled to write another book, *Experience and Education* [9], because of his unhappiness with the way in which his views of education were being translated into action by his followers. What American progressive educators got wrong was their over-correction of the excesses of traditional schooling; if schools paid too little attention to the child's needs, the progressives too often over-emphasised those needs. If traditional classrooms were rigidly organised, the progressives were overly-skittish about imposing any order at all. If traditional education was tied too tightly to prespecified courses of study, the progressives too often would simply allow it all to 'emerge'. If traditional education neglected matters of meaning and personal significance, the progressives emphasised, to a fault, the need to teach only what the child decided he wanted to learn. If traditional schooling placed too much emphasis on grades and marks, the progressives steered away from evaluating the quality of the student's work. What Dewey saw, to his dismay, was a form of progressive education that developed its agenda primarily by reacting against the prevailing system of schooling, a system that did in fact often neglect the particularities of child development.

But as Dewey pointed out, and it is a lesson well worth re-learning today, the amelioration of rigidity is not located in *laissez-faire* schooling. Nor is a solution to be found by following a middle of the road policy. What one must do is to build a conception of educational practice upon an adequate conception of experience. For experience to have educational significance, the individual should develop from it the ability to cope intelligently with the problems he will invariably encounter in the world. For art educators, it is the arts, and the visual arts in particular, that provide the occasions for those problems. Programmes of art education that have a significant educational yield for children enable them to think more intelligently about art and its various manifestations in the world. Providing experience that helps children learn how to think about art is what the disciplines in discipline-based art education are intended to accomplish. And just what are they to learn? What kinds of problems do they encounter when they engage art? Just what do people do with art?

There are four major things that people do with art. They make it. They look at it. They understand its place in culture over time. They make judgements about its quality. In discipline-based art education these four operations constitute art production, art criticism, art history and aesthetics. Art production helps children learn to think intelligently about the creation of visual images. It helps them learn how to create images that have expressive power, coherence, insight, and ingenuity. Art criticism develops their ability to see, not merely to look at, the qualities that constitute the visual world—a world that includes, yet exceeds, formal works of art. Art history helps children to understand something of the place and time within which all works of art are situated. No art form exists in a de-contextualised vacuum: a part of the meaning of any work depends upon understanding its context.

17

Aesthetics—the newest entry in art education's curricular arena—pertains to the theoretical bases for judging the quality of what one sees. Human beings are evaluative creatures. We argue about our value judgements and we are keen to make them. Understanding the variety of criteria that can be applied to works of art, and reflecting about the meanings of that intellectually delicious and elusive concept 'art' is what much of aesthetics is about. Discipline-based art education is intended to expand the child's ability to cope with problems in each of these four domains.

The realisation of these educational intentions depends upon the existence of curricula that give children access to the experiences just described. It also depends upon the abilities of teachers to mediate intelligently the programmes that are provided. Without substantive curricula, the child's educational experience will be shallow. Without intelligent teaching, the benefits of substantive curricula will simply remain dormant. We need both curricula worth teaching and teachers sufficiently skilled to make their potential a reality in classrooms. Just how can our programmes be structured so these aims are achieved? And just what do we mean by the term 'structure'? Because curricula are so important in realising our educational aims, I will focus my remarks first on the meaning of 'structure' and then on the structural elements that can be used to design different kinds of curricula meeting *DBAE* criteria.

First the term 'structure'. One common meaning, and one that I reject, is the view that structure refers to a tightly designed set of goals and procedures that controls the student's behaviour and severely limits his options. When parents say that their child needs a highly structured environment, this is often what they mean. But structure, in my view, pertains to the way things are related. All forms, except perhaps the most chaotic, have some structure, some set of coherent relationships among their components. Curricula are no exceptions. Curricula are plans, activities and materials that are intended to influence the learner's experience. How these plans are designed, what these activities are to be, what materials are to be employed, are products of educational decision-making that are contingent upon the values to which we subscribe and the options we can envision.

What are the structural options that are available in the design of *DBAE*? Consider first the *boundary strength* between art and other subjects within the elementary school curriculum [10]. One way to design an art curriculum is to differentiate it clearly from everything else that is taught. To pursue this form of curriculum planning means that art will have its own place on the educational agenda as a separate but equal subject, like the other subjects that students encounter. Here the integrity of the subject is maintained by protecting it from dilution with other subjects: art is not meant to serve as handmaiden to the social studies or the language arts. Time each week is allocated to the visual arts, or to music, dance, or drama, and these subjects are taught in curricular forms not much different than mathematics or reading—only less often.

The degree to which the subjects that constitute the school's curriculum are bounded and insulated from each other is variable. Even self-contained classrooms can have a curriculum whose subjects have strong boundaries. Designing curricula with little boundary strength is also an option that imaginative curriculum planners can pursue. One can imagine programmes in which the visual arts are taught in relation to history or the language arts. Here boundary strength is diminished and flexibility is emphasised. Many primary school teachers prefer programmes that attempt to provide the child with a less fragmented, more integrated approach to the content they study. When courses of study make connections between subjects, fragmentation is diminished and integration is fostered.

The integration of one subject with others is not without potential costs. When integration is aimed at, the special features of a subject are often compromised in the process. On balance, I favour a stronger boundary strength for the arts in order to protect their special characteristics from being swamped by subjects often regarded as more important. In saying this I am taking a position. Yet I do recognise that any approach has its trade-offs. I value integration, coherence and unity. I would urge that connections between the arts and other subjects be made when they can, as long as the values of art are not diminished in the process. My main point here, the subtext of the text, is that the structure of curriculum for discipline-based art education is itself an open issue. I have my own predilection, but there is no structural orthodoxy to which all must subscribe. The critical issue is to achieve the educational aims to which *DBAE* is committed.

Thus far I have commented about a curriculum structure that differentially insulates subjects from others. The degree of boundary strength between subjects is only one of the structural elements that can be varied in curriculum planning. The degree of *within-subject integration* is also a planning option. In discipline-based art education the four disciplines, art production, art criticism, art history, and aesthetics, can be treated as integrated or as insulated elements. Art production can be taught with little or no attention to art history or to aesthetics, and criticism can be taught with little or no attention to art production. The four disciplines that constitute *DBAE* can run as independent, parallel courses, or as integrated components of a core unit or activity that is designed to illuminate the relationships between concepts, skills and generalisations within the four fields.

In the case of within-subject relationships, I prefer art curricula whose constituent disciplines are, on the whole, integrated. The reason for my preference is that I believe art history, art criticism, and even aesthetics, take on greater meaning for students if they are related to their own productive work. A student who has worked on the problem of creating virtual movement in a painting is more likely to find meaning in the works of Bridget Riley, Marcel Duchamp, and the Futurists, than one who has not. The motives of these artists' interest in virtual movement can be examined and the different ways in which they resolved the problems they set for themselves can be understood.

In suggesting the heuristic potential of painting in making these

connections, I am not suggesting that productive activities are the only
vehicles through which connections can be made. The reading of
primary source material—for example, the opinions of critics who

commented on the early Cézanne, Seurat, or Bonnard—are rich resources for understanding how cultural-historical values affect the perception and appraisal of art. Writing of Cézanne, one nineteenth century critic commented:

> In his works he is a Greek of the great period; his canvases have the calm and heroic serenity of the paintings and terra cottas of antiquity, and the ignorant who laugh at the *Bathers*, for example, seem to me like barbarians criticizing the Parthenon. [Another critic,] André Perate, while admiring much about Cézanne, thought his sketches . . . merely childish. Others wrote that his drawing was like that of a 'clumsy child' and the style of his work peurile and childish [11].

6 PAUL CÉZANNE *Bathers (La Grande Baignade)*, 1898–1905, oil on canvas 82 × 98·25"; Philadelphia Museum of Art, © ADAGP, Paris & DACS, London, 1989. (photo: W.P Wilstach Collection)

Comments such as these can provide important intellectual stimuli for challenging students' opinions about the nature of art; enter aesthetic theory. Here art criticism, art history and aesthetics can be joined.

At present, I know of no published text that provides such provocative materials for high school art students.

My comments thus far have focused on the variability of boundary-strength as a structural feature of discipline-based art education curricula. What can also vary is the degree to which the framing of curricular events is located in the heads and hands of curriculum writers or is under the control of teachers and students. Framing pertains to who controls what, how and when something is to be taught. In American educational planning, we tend to align ourselves with one camp or another. Either the teacher controls everything or the teacher controls nothing. Either the teacher decides what, how and when something will be taught, or the teacher is scrupulously to follow the written curriculum. In the latter case, content, activity, sequence, and aims are all prescribed. Once on the track, the teacher is expected to complete the journey to its final destination, and the ride often takes forty weeks.

But it is clear that curricula cannot prescribe all that a teacher is to do; we have learned enough from the efforts to design teacher-proof curricula to avoid such naïve aspirations. Curricula can provide space for teacher judgement and interpretation in at least two locations. First, they can invite teachers to create their own activities instrumental to particular *DBAE* goals. Second, they need not try to fill out each of the American school year's forty weeks with curriculum activities. Teachers can work with curriculum material designed for smaller time units. As a matter of fact, I would urge that teachers take on three curriculum units during the school year. Each unit might last only one month. The second year the teacher can add another three units; the third year another three. The implementation of a *DBAE* curriculum is no one-year effort; three to five years is more like it. In short, the framing of curricular activities need not be modelled after recipes for baking brownies. We need not, and do not now have a cookbook theory of curriculum planning. Curriculum planners can intentionally provide teachers and their students with opportunities to frame some of their own activities and aims.

Let me now turn to matters of sequence in an art curriculum. Some in our field argue that unlike mathematics or the language arts, in the visual arts sequence is not a primary curricular consideration. I reject such a view. In the first place sequence is inevitable; all activities in any programme exist over time. In that sense alone there must be a sequence to the activities that students engage in: it is an ineluctable function of time. But in a more psychological sense, sequence pertains to the organisation of activities so that they challenge, develop, and build upon the ideas and skills that students have previously acquired. Programmes that have no sequential development are programmes that are educationally static. One of the best ways to ensure a lack of movement is to have students work with so many materials that they are unable to make connections between what they have learned at one point in time and what they are dealing with at another.

Far too many art programmes have precisely such characteristics. Sequence, therefore, is not only inevitable: when intelligently designed it builds upon what students have learned and prepares them for what is to come. It helps students internalise the content of their experiences. This internalisation is more likely if the curriculum activities give students ample opportunities to practise ideas and skills. For example, if students are asked to describe metaphorically the expressive qualities of a work of art, say a particular work of architecture, they can be asked to do the same for sculpture, painting, graphics, ceramics, and, eventually, for the streets on which they live, the advertisements they see in magazines, and the people they know. We have typically been so concerned with providing variety in our curriculum that sequence and continuity have often been neglected. Doing less may well result in achieving more.

There is another reason why sequence and continuity are important in discipline-based art education curricula. That reason has to do with *automaticity*. Automaticity pertains to the internalisation of learning so that one can employ skills or call upon ideas without conscious effort. Our driving skills have been automatised. We can talk, listen to music, or let our minds wander and still manage to get home on time. We can dance without thinking about which foot goes where. We have so acquired language that we need not labour to say what is on our minds— at least in English.

In the arts automaticity allows students to attend to aesthetic matters because matters of technical control have been mastered. When a student has to focus his attention on keeping the material under control, imaginative possibilities and aesthetic considerations must take a back seat. When a student has to struggle to recall the meaning and features of the Baroque, the ability to use this concept as a basis for discussion, debate, and comparison is remote. Automaticity is what confers freedom to our imagination. Its development in our cognitive repertoire depends upon programmes designed to provide for sequence and continuity. Without sequence, ideas and skills are less likely to become more complex and sophisticated. Without continuity they are unlikely to be internalised. Any curriculum structure for *DBAE* must, in my opinion, provide for the development of such skills.

My major aim thus far has been to identify some of the structural elements that can be varied in the creation of *DBAE* curricula. There is no single set of sanctified programmes that those of us interested in *DBAE* are obliged to employ. What should be sought are programmes with substance that will give children access to a stunning part of their culture. This should serve as an invitation to encourage LEAs and local cultural institutions, foundations, and government agencies to join hands and minds in the creation of resources that will assist the teacher. Good curriculum materials both guide and liberate. They guide because they model and suggest content, activities, and aims that teachers might not consider on their own. They liberate because good materials not only teach students, they also teach teachers. They enable teachers, over time, to free themselves from the constraints of materials designed by others, and to design their own, by their own lights, for their own students. Like all deep learning, with a genuinely excellent curriculum, the teacher becomes a kind of virtuoso, someone who can exploit virtually any option to do something educationally effective with students. A Utopian view? Perhaps. But I believe one worth aiming at.

This brings me to my final remarks about discipline-based art education. I have said a fair amount about structure, but what about magic? The magic is located in what art can do to us if we know how to read its form. After all is said and done, art criticism, art history, and aesthetics are, in my view, instruments for securing the experience that art makes possible. What art provides is a two-fold contribution to human development and human experience. First art, by which I mean images and events whose structural properties elicit aesthetic forms of feeling, is one of the important means through which the potentialities of the human mind are brought into being. Our intellectual capacities become intellectual abilities as we give these capacities opportunities to function. The kind of thinking that is required to see what is subtle and complex, to learn how to attend to forms so that their expressive structure engages our emotion and imagination, to tolerate—indeed pursue—the enigmatic ambiguities of art, contribute to the development of some of our most complex cognitive skills. Far from being a mindless activity, our engagement with art calls upon our most subtle and complex forms of perception.

A second contribution of the arts pertains to the kind of meaning that art makes possible. Education is an enterprise whose general aim is to expand the forms of literacy that individuals can employ. By literacy I mean the ability to represent or recover meaning in the variety of forms through which it is made public. In our culture, words, numbers, movements, images, and patterns of sound are forms through which meaning is represented. To read those forms requires an understanding of their rules, their contexts, and their syntactical structures. Each form of representation imposes its own limits and provides its own possibilities.

Some meanings are better expressed in visual images, others in movement; some meanings require the use of propositions, others the use of number. Indeed each of these forms of representation was invented to do what the others could not do. Each has its own sphere or realm of meaning—witness the photographic images of Dorothea Lang, the sculpture of Henry Moore, the poetry of Cummings, the dance of Martha Graham or George Balanchine. Artistic literacy is the means we use to experience the meaning that the works of these artists make possible. Works of art convey the ineffable. They cultivate the sensibilities so that the subtle is seen, the covert is counted. In a word, art helps us to know what we cannot articulate. To the extent to which schools are aimed at helping students *know*, the arts are potent educational resources. The development of mind and the generation of insight are two critically important contributions of art, but where, oh where, is the magic?

No analysis of art or justification of its role would be adequate if it neglected the pleasures of art *per se*. Art has the magical capacities to send us to the moon. Like a rocket it can make our pulse beat faster, it can bring a flush to our face, it can create a rush that is its own reward. The sensuous surface of a Dan mask, the elegance of a Zapotec figure, the energy of a De Kooning image, the sheer power of a Beethoven symphony, the poetic passion of a Shakespearian couplet, are simply exquisite forms of human experience—magical, captivating, self-justifying.

To understand what I mean, think about the images that have changed your life. Those that have changed mine are El Greco's *Assumption of the Virgin* at the top of the great stairway in the Art Institute of Chicago; Willem De Kooning's black paintings; a Senufo rhythm pounder, made by an anonymous African sculptor, in the Helena Rubenstein Collection; the bronze *Poseidon*, salvaged from the sea, that now stands in the National Museum of Art in Athens; the final movement of Beethoven's *Ninth Symphony*; the acres of cemetery headstones and miles of desperate tenements that I see from the window of my cab as I travel from New York's Kennedy Airport to Manhattan; and a small eighth century Chancay effigy in a corner of a dimly lit gallery in London's British Museum.

These are the images that have sent me to the moon. Which images have sent you on your trip? No art programme devoid of such experience, or that fails to open the door to it, completes its ultimate mission. No door can be opened without a curriculum having both structure and magic. Without structure in our curriculum, we get no automaticity. With no automaticity we get no internalisation. With no internalisation, we get no magic. Those who worry about the deadening potential of structure, I hope will be reassured that those of us committed to discipline-based art education are also committed to magic. Without it there is no art. Without structure there is no access.

Notes and References

1 BARKAN, MANUEL. 1962. Transitions in Art Education, *Art Education*, 15, 7; October.
2 LANIER, VINCENT. 1963. Schizmogenesis in Art Education, *Studies in Art Education*, 5, 1.
3 EISNER, ELLIOT. 1968. Curriculum Making for the Wee Folk: Stanford University's Kettering Project, *Studies in Art Education*, 9, 3.
4 MILLS, ANDREW E and D ROSS THOMSON. 1987. *A National Art(s) Education 1984–5*. Reston, Virginia, National Art Education Association.
5 One of the most important sources of support, and my reason for cautious optimism, is to be found in the efforts of *The J Paul Getty Center for Education and the Arts*. The Center has had the intelligence and the guts to take on a difficult job with sensitivity and insight, and, to my mind, with effect. It has elected to work with professionals committed to the long-term improvement of the arts in education. It seeks no orthodoxy in method, but it has recognised the need to work within the system, not to bypass it. It has focused its efforts on the fundamentals of curriculum and teaching, not simply on the sexy and superficial.
6 HAMBLEN, KAREN. 1985. The Issue of Technocratic Rationality in Discipline-Based Art Education, *Studies In Art Education*, 27, 1, p. 45.
7 HAUSMAN, JEROME. 1985. Review of: *Beyond Creating: the Place for Art in American Schools*. Los Angeles, The J Paul Getty Trust Fund, p. 153.
8 DEWEY, JOHN. 1902. *The Child and the Curriculum*. Chicago U.P., pp. 14–15.

9   DEWEY, JOHN. 1938. *Experience and Education*. New York, Collier Books.
10 See BERNSTEIN, BASIL. 1971. On the Classification and Framing of
    Educational Knowlege, in: MICHAEL YOUNG (ed) *Knowledge and Control:
    New Directions for the School of Education*. London, Macmillan.
11 HAMILTON, GEORGE H. 1977. Cézanne and his Critics, in: WILLIAM RUBIN
    (ed) *Cézanne: The Late Works*. New York, MOMA pp. 140–2.

Chapter Three

ROD TAYLOR Critical Studies in Art and Design Education: Passing Fashion or the Missing Element?

The National *Critical Studies in Art Education Project* (CSAE), which ran from 1981 to 1984, undoubtedly raised levels of consciousness about the place and role of *Critical Studies* in art and design education. It arose out of a growing concern that the predominant emphasis on practical activity meant that the majority of pupils were leaving school with little or no knowledge and understanding of the visual arts other than that acquired solely through their own practice. Numerous art educators, both here and in North America, had articulated the strong case for *Critical Studies* and most syllabuses and schemes of work contained aims about 'making pupils aware of their cultural heritage' and introducing them to artists, craftspeople and their work, both past and present. In reality, though, there was little evidence of these theoretical justifications and aims leading to systematic classroom practices designed to realise them. Some of the all-too-rare examples that were identified by the CSAE I have documented elsewhere [1]. The Project argued and demonstrated that both primary and secondary pupils could appreciate and enjoy a variety of art and craft objects in their own right, and understand them in context, when the educational approaches were appropriate. It also illustrated how pupils of all ages could make beneficial links between their own practical needs and their growing awareness of the works of others, whether by their own peers or by mature artists.

There has subsequently been a considerable and gratifying amount of school and gallery-based *Critical Studies* activity; and some, at least, of the approaches that are being developed are likely to become established practice in the coming years. It now seems certain that, for the first time, most courses to sixteen-plus level will contain a *Critical Studies* component: this will terminate the trend in recent years which has led to only a small, academically-élite group of A-level students being deemed capable of practising the subject and also studying it to any depth. This is, of course, largely because of the recognition of the significance of *Critical Studies* at GCSE level, with its stipulations about course content and expressions of assessment objectives such as Number Nine of the Northern Examining Association, which reads:

> Candidates will be expected to demonstrate the ability to make
> informed responses to contemporary and historical art and design
> through an awareness of artistic qualities, an analysis and evaluation
> of design, and the forming and expressing of judgements [2].

Any lingering doubts should be further expelled now that the *Draft Grade Criteria Report* of the Art and Design Working Party has been published. A decade ago few people could have envisaged a report of this nature. It identifies three domains which in total are fundamental to any 'in the round' art and design course. These are the *conceptual*, the *productive*, and the *contextual and critical*, and following their introduction candidates will be expected to demonstrate some levels of competence in each in order to obtain a Grade E or above [3]. A-level boards are also reviewing their syllabuses in the light of GCSE National Criteria, meaning that a *Critical Studies* component should eventually be a characteristic of all the courses on offer at this level. Having seen the motivating effects of *Critical Studies* on their fourth year pupils and on their own teaching, an increasing number of teachers are now introducing the subject to their first year pupils on entry. There are also significant developments being generated within the primary sector. The introduction of the GCSE is therefore giving added momentum to *Critical Studies* developments (already set in motion by the CSAE Project): these are extending back into the early school-years, and they are bound to project forward into further and higher education.

Though designed as assessment tools the three domains, when fully recognised and taken into account by teachers, have the potential to benefit the whole of a teacher's practice. The GCSE, with its increased emphasis on course content and creative process, will substantially widen assessment procedures that have formerly had very narrow parameters. The long-standing examination emphasis on skill and technique—in other words, the myopic exclusive concern for the *productive* domain— all too often led to cliché art and predictability. The crumpled Coke can, the half pepper, cabbage and cauliflower, the endless squaring-up and copying from pop-star photographs, and the reduction of art and design to colour, line, tone and texture exercises are all increasingly being seen as symbols of this sole obsession.

Inevitably, it seems, some of these lessons have simply been adapted. In the name of *Critical Studies*, the postcard reproduction and the photocopier may both provide pupils with images to debase by reducing them to the same old colour, line, tone and texture lessons. Surely the *contextual and critical* domain implies and means more than this! There is immeasurable difference between such studies as ends in themselves, and work which genuinely relates to pupils' own practical needs. Joe, now a well-known Rugby League star, was an A-level student in Wigan at the time of the *Gerd Winner and Kelpra Studio* exhibition at the *Drumcroon Education Art Centre* [4]. The impact of Winner's work was so great that he discarded Degas as his chosen 'personal study' topic in order to write about Winner instead. Having seen more of the artist's work in the Print Room of the Tate Gallery, he observed:

> Certainly, back in Wigan, walking round, a brick wall would now be a Winner wall, if you looked at it right, and a lamp post stood out rather than just being something at the side of a road. You came to look as a camera might, you'd walk round and see with Winner's eyes, just walking. Especially when you went to the canals and warehouses, the fire escapes seemed to be more prominent. You seemed to get a totally different viewpoint [5].

7   A Gerd Winner screenprint from *London East One*, Drumcroon Education Arts Centre, Wigan

8   A Wigan brick wall 'would be a Winner wall, if you looked at it right...', Drumcroon Education Arts Centre, Wigan.

One could not have a clearer example of heightened environmental awareness, and it is important because it represents a bridging link between the study of other people's art and one's own practice. Its relevance can be as significant for much younger pupils, and is reflected in the responses of 10-year-olds during the same Winner exhibition. Their images of the Wigan Pier area, prior to its recent redevelopment, reveal an unusual intensity of observation which arises out of their contact with the artist, their understanding of, and insight into, his work. The scales have been removed from their eyes and they see the type of environment which they have walked through every day of their lives as if for the first time. The parallels between Winner's depictions of *London East One* and their renderings of their urban environment are unmistakable, and are equally reflected in the abundance of written work that was also generated. One pupil, for example, wrote:

A railway seeks its way through a smoky cloud. Suddenly a train shoots past making a hissing clicking sound. As we walked it was like a never ending town of houses, factories, warehouses and a labyrinth of roads. The main road was ominous. We went under a dark dismal bridge that carried trains over our heads. Lots of towering shops and buildings surrounded us. Moving under bridges, over bridges, through bridges. Past broken-down factories, warehouses and mills. Iron bars in the lifting equipment were rusty and the water underneath was carrying away the rust [6].

These young people, once so affected, become aware of a new range of possibilities relevant to their own art making. On first becoming aware of Degas through slide examples Anne recreated his typical motifs in her bedroom, leading to a series of paintings and drypoint etchings of great intensity. She said:

. . . it helps you in your work to study the painters—it's helped me. It's given me more ideas about what to do. Before you'd just see something outside like the buildings, and you'd just draw that. You look at things differently now. Things that you wouldn't have found interesting before, now you do. It's changed the way that I look at things [7].

In its definition of the *contextual and critical* domain, the *Draft Grade Criteria Report* emphasises that it is concerned with 'a developing awareness of [pupils'] own work and that of others' [8]. This helps us envisage a continuum from the work of each pupil to that of his or her peers, and then eventually to 'great' art, embracing folk, popular and other ethnic arts, all the crafts and every area of design. Anne, therefore becomes friendly with Sheila and Nikki through their related art endeavours, and the efforts and ideas of each affirm and enrich the practice of the others [9].

Samantha further illustrates in the most vivid manner how insights, developed through increased critical awareness, can dramatically change a young person's concepts and consequently her whole approach to personal work. An O-level art and design failure, she only began A-levels in her second year Sixth and by her own testimony was unmotivated and underachieving, employing a range of excuses to work away from the studios and to avoid producing her inadequate sketchbook on request. At the commencement of the third year Sixth, though, she was introduced to fifteenth century Flemish painting and her interest turned to fascination and love when she saw examples in the original in the National Gallery. In the van Eyck *Arnolfini Marriage* painting she felt that

> You got a peep of the world outside of the window . . . and you could see the fashions of then. You know, and the shoes and the little dog and the little mirror at the back where you could see the artist. I don't know, there was so much in the painting; I like quite a lot going on in paintings really [10].

She was attracted by the detail, by the pristine surface of the panel and the jewel-like richness of the colour, and she was fascinated by the symbolism. She saw a connection between the hands of the praying donors, who recurred in a number of the panels, and her own feet (the main features in a painting she had just commenced, based on a sketchbook study drawn at home). She bought reproductions for her folder and bedroom wall, and she was conscious of attempting to emulate some of their characteristics in her painting of her feet. She described the results as her treasure into which she had put her thoughts and feelings. For the first time she was not embarrassed to acknowledge her work. 'In fact, you'd bring your friends in and say "Look what I've done!" It was a really lovely feeling.' Every painting produced that year featured her feet, to which she referred as her 'signature'.

In response to the examination topic *Modern Morality* she used her mother and her sister's friend as models. Both were at prayer, one—the mother—unquestioning about her faith, in a conventional praying posture with hands together and eyes firmly shut. The younger model, however, was 'withstanding the pressures of the church', desiring to lead her life in her own way. Her hands were clenched, the rosary beads entwined between the fingers.

> The rosary beads stood for the church and as it was intertwined it meant that she was tied to the church to a certain degree and her look is one of frightened distance, really, with her mother sitting behind. Her expression is very clamped. The mouth is tight, the wrinkles are harsh and the hands are pressed together as if insisting 'I do believe.' The young girl seemed to be questioning—looking away—but she *is* tied to her mother's feelings and the church. She has respect and duty to the mother but also respect for herself.

Her interest in the symbolism of Flemish painting was made manifest and her love of those donors had now surfaced in a clear and decisive manner. However, she had to include her 'signature'! She did this by including the feet of a crucifix in the top right-hand corner of the preliminary drawing. In addition, she made a powerfully expressive drawing of just these feet. But how on earth had she achieved the effect of the nails penetrating the flesh? Surely she could not have simply imagined this!

> Well you see, we have this big deep freeze at home and I got my dad to get this big lump of pork and he hammered two bolts into it for

31

me. I got my sister to stand on her toes until the veins stood out in her feet and then I painted the stigmata onto her feet with cochineal.

9   Samantha's drawing for *Modern Morality*, Drumcroon Education Arts Centre, Wigan.

By using her imagination she just 'put the two together.' This previously unmotivated student had produced this extraordinary study for a small detail in her painting-to-be which she could so easily have fudged. In the painting the symbolism was further extended into colour, with 'the red for the Mary Magdalene and the blue on her mum for the Virgin Mary.'

The *Draft Grade Criteria Report* stipulates:

> Candidates should show evidence of their knowledge and understanding of the different contexts in which work may be produced (eg. historical, social, cultural, technological and a developing ability to make informed critical judgements [11].

Most art and design courses in recent years have been lacking in such characteristics. Nevertheless, the bridging of fifteenth century Flemish values and Samantha's contemporary concerns imbues her work with an historical dimension, and it is also overlaid with social, cultural, moral and religious values. Her love of Flemish art is the crucial element which enables her to invest her own work with these qualities: the *contextual and critical* has a direct bearing on the *conceptual*, which in turn gives meaning to what she undertakes in the *productive* realm.

32

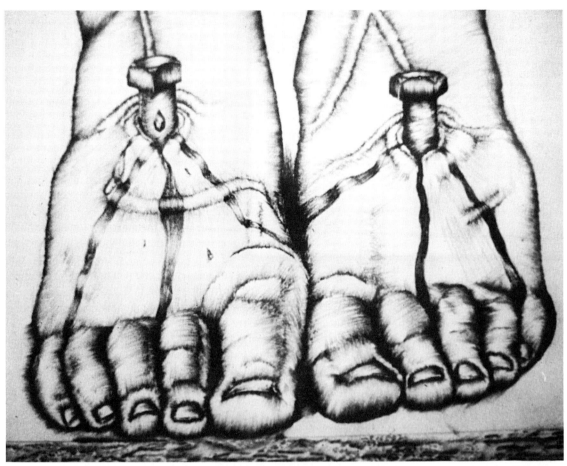

10 Samantha's drawing of feet for use in *Modern Morality*, Drumcroon Education Arts Centre, Wigan.

Even quite young children are capable of unravelling the symbolic meaning of complex works, and of relating to them at significant levels. A Wigan exhibition entitled *Pierre Degen: New Work* included body sculptures which the artist called 'Personal Environments'. Many adult visitors were completely baffled but Sandra, a third year Junior, became intrigued by them.

> In Pierre Degen's exhibition there was this Personal Environment No. 3 . . . I spent a lot of time talking to Pierre about [this] because I like it. When I was looking at this Personal Environment it was shaped like a little world of your own. It had red cloth, yellow dowel, black cloth, blue and white string, and white cloth. First of all I thought this is going to be hard to understand and then I found out that the red was for sunset, yellow dowel was for the sun, the black cloth was for night, the blue and white string was for the sky and last of all the white cloth was for the morning. Pierre Degen did not think that until I told him [12].

Sandra had devised a logic in which the curtained environment opened and closed in response to the occupant's moods. Her teacher recalls Degen saying to Sandra 'I never looked at it like that until you told me.'

In a related workshop session she decided, not surprisingly, to relate her three-dimensional construction to *Personal Environment No. 3*.

> I wanted to make mine a bit the same, but I didn't want to use a lot of cloth hanging down or else I wouldn't be able to see where I were going, so I just thought I'd make it down one side instead of all around me. It was a bit sore on my shoulder when I wore it because of the harness. It was just plonked on there, and I had to hold a stick at the front of it, and it was hard to keep hold of that and keep it on my shoulder. I had to turn sideways going through a door or my environment it would just have gone splat, and the wood would have broke at the side. I were a bit worried in case I banged somebody in the back. It was a bit too big you see.

What a wonderful example of a design-related activity for a primary school child! The engagement with a mature artist's work enabled Sandra to become involved in a variety of activities, on a scale and with processes which are relatively uncommon in the primary—or for that matter, the secondary—phase of education. However important these practical interactions are, though, there should always be scope for young people to enjoy the work of others in its own right. It is my belief that they should, of right, leave school having acquired a sense of enjoyment as well as knowledge and understanding about aspects of the wider world of the visual arts. For example, David, a fourth year GCSE pupil, is attracted to the way David Hepher 'uses the buildings to control the people' in his paintings, expressing 'a subtle social comment.'

> The painting which I have chosen is 'Camberwell Flats 2'. I have chosen this because of its fine quality of texture and shape. The painting is a detailed study of one section, one society, one little bit of Camberwell Flats. But even though it is only one section of the flats you get the feeling and atmosphere of the entire buildings.
> The painting is made up of five floors. There is a different feel about every one, but the change is subtly done. All David Hepher's work is subtle, not stating a definite thought, but a composition of thoughts scattered through the paintings, to which a person viewing the picture will come to his own conclusion.
> Each 'segment' is individual, projecting the gossip and life of each of the inhabitants' daily activities. The highest floor has a little boy dangling his feet through the safety fence. I think for me anyway, this is the story of the whole painting. This is how I feel:
>
> *I could jump if I want, but what's the point in jumping,*
> *I could fall, but why am I falling:*
> *It would be in the same death list*
> *What would I miss if I fell now.*
>
> Another clever aspect of Hepher's work is the fact that he always introduces another element, despite what's going on in the flats. This element (on the Camberwell Flats, it is the edge of the brick of a house) does not intrude, on the main picture, it merely gives a perspective, an extra perspective, looking at the flats at a different angle, from another world, like one particular tribe looking

anxiously to the other, 'I wonder what it would be like?' . . . that sort of thing [13].

Irrespective of whether there are any practical consequences or not, David's gallery-based responses to Hepher's painting reveals a sensitivity to its mood, form and content which is a valuable experience in its own right, and one which has been denied to too many young people for too long.

These innovations in art and design education are obviously challenging and they are inevitably causing consternation in some quarters, particularly as they are receiving an ever-increasing acceptance. There are some who find it difficult to reconcile *Critical Studies* with long-cherished child-centred approaches. Maurice Barrett, for example, argues that *Critical Studies* might be valid for the over-thirteens but not for younger children, and that the work of mature artists has relevance to validate what pupils have done, but should only be introduced in the wake of practical activities [14]. There is currently a *Critical Studies* lobby, he suggests, and all lobbyists are distorters! [15] It is still common to hear it stated that *Critical Studies* is a bandwagon, and an American import at that! In the light of such observations, it is intriguing to realise how consistent have been the attitudes of leading British art educators (many closely associated with child-centred developments) over the last half century or so. Many have been important 'lobbyists' in their time, contributing to the subject's shift away from renderings of acanthus leaves and perspective drawings of wooden blocks: their views are therefore of considerable significance.

11, 12 Figure drawings by Ian and Neil, aged 11, produced at the Drumcroon Saturday morning classes, Drumcroon Education Arts Centre, Wigan.

13   The Drumroon Gallery showing the use of supporting contextual material. Boxer, the *Animal Farm* horse, has been made by primary children for eventual siting at Wigan North Western Railway Station, Drumcroon Education Arts Centre, Wigan.

As long ago as 1937 Herbert Read was suggesting that
  . . . the number of those to be trained in the appreciation of art
  should be vastly increased . . . for common sense as well as
  psychology tells us that the aesthetic impulses . . . are the normal

possession of children [16].

In 1947 R R Tomlinson was pointing out that

> Environment can and does have a profound effect . . . upon the
> form which concepts take. It is therefore of great importance that
> children should be acquainted with the world's great art and craft in
> addition to well-designed things of modern manufacture [17].

A year later Marion Richardson was recommending

> . . . surrounding the children, as far as possible, with reproductions
> of great pictures of all sorts. In this good company taste will have
> had the opportunity of developing unconsciously, and can prove an
> armour of defence,

because, she said, the sincerity of great art parallels that of children,

> . . . and they can dimly feel it as a bond and common
> denominator [18].

Seonaid Robertson echoed these sentiments in 1963, suggesting that

> Only through a sincere study of the masters (both old and
> contemporary) as people doing the same sort of thing as himself . . .
> will he grow from childhood to manhood in art, with expression and
> appreciation interweaving. So can a child and an adolescent grow
> into his own culture and root his present in its past [19].

Again in 1963 Sybil Marshall too appreciated this relationship between
the work of the mature artist and the pupil's needs:

> To be able to approach the classic works of art without fear, and
> with pleasure, interest, understanding and love is to be able to tap
> the inexhaustible well of past human experience [20].

At numerous conferences since 1981 I have heard it suggested that it
is Marion Richardson and her like who are responsible for the mess art
and design education is in. It is they, the argument goes, who in prizing
children's innocence, spontaneity, imagination and ideas, have divorced
children's art from all other, in the process denying them the means to
nurture and stimulate the imagination. The unanimity expressed in the
above quotations is therefore of the utmost importance. It is not she but
her supposed followers, in their misreadings and misinterpretations, who
have done harm, reducing the teacher to the role of passive non-
interventionist. There are always honourable exceptions of course. No-
one is more sensitive to children's stages of development than Keith
Gentle, but he is also aware that

> It is when they become more serious and discerning about their own
> image making that they can focus on the particular way in which
> images are constructed. The ability to 'read' sophisticated images is
> clearly something which children can learn to do with considerable
> personal enrichment . . . [21].

Obviously there will always be areas of disagreement. Whereas Marion
Richardson sought to surround her children with 'reproductions of great
pictures of all sorts', Herbert Read was emphatic that

> Children should, of course, be shown the work of mature artists,
> both of the past and of the present (and preferably not
> reproductions) [22].

This argument about the relative merits of primary and secondary source material continues and will no doubt persist into the future. It is surely significant, though, (minor differences notwithstanding) that these leading authorities have been united in their agreement about the importance of children engaging the work of mature artists. Few would doubt that, given the opportunity, Marion Richardson would have preferred her pupils to have seen her beloved Post-Impressionist paintings in the original.

Today there is an acceptance that a wide variety of original, and not only 'great', works are worthy of study, and that the impact of experiencing works in the original is of a different order and intensity, convenient though reproductions are [23]. But it is how such resources are used that really counts: there is a real problem in the fact that the educations of many teachers themselves have focused on art production, with the critical aspects neglected even at BA level. This dilemma was summarised by Jane, a PGCE student, who had gone right through the art education system only to realise that her knowledge of art history and appreciation was minimal.

> . . . I resigned myself to the fact that each painting or art object must have one particular correct interpretation and meaning, and I was far too ignorant and lowly to contradict this: my place was to agree with the 'answer' to the work, not contribute and certainly not to criticise it. The one unchallengeable interpretation would be found in books or on television by art critics and must be learnt, if my appreciation were to improve. Horrified and scared by this dreary prospect, I shut my mind off and decided to suffer in silence [24].

Fortunately this student did benefit appreciably from positive, remedial PGCE support. I was reminded of her, though, when a teacher suddenly exclaimed at an LEA conference

> There's just one thing I'd like to know. *What do you actually say to pupils when you are standing in front of a painting?*

She probably put into words an inhibition felt by many. But the growing acceptance that we should think in terms of *histories* of art, as Arthur Hughes emphasises [25], can give teachers—and in turn their pupils—the confidence to engage in fruitful conjecture in front of art objects without Jane's fear of being wrong. Even without prior knowledge of a work, it can still be approached from four fundamental standpoints, each with the potential of generating a wide range of discussion, questioning and responses. These are *content, form, process,* and *mood,* and they give rise to the following kinds of question:

CONTENT

What is the work about? What is its subject-matter? Is the subject-matter incidental or is it, for example, a vehicle for the social, religious, moral or political concerns of either artist or client? Was the subject-matter observed directly, remembered or imagined? Has it been treated representationally or is there deliberate exaggeration, distortion or abstraction? If so, why? Is the subject-matter surface deep or are there hidden, or not immediately apparent, meanings alluded to through the use of, for example, symbols, analogies, metaphors?

FORM

How has the work been arranged? Is this in keeping with its content? Does it confirm or contradict the work's imagery? What kind of colour scheme has been used? Is it, for example, harmonious or is it one of contrasts? Does one colour dominate or do two or more have equal significance? Is there one principal shape or is it composed of inter-relating combinations of shapes? Are there recurring shapes, lines, rhythms, forms, etc., which determine the design of the work? Does the work have variety or unity of texture? Does the work hold together as an overall entity, or is it pleasing in parts yet unsatisfactory as a whole?

PROCESS

How was the work made and what was it made with? What materials, tools, processes and techniques did the artist use? How and where might the artist have commenced the work? Through what stages might the work have proceeded from commencement to completion? Might the artist have made supporting studies—sketches, photographs, maquettes, collages or stencils for example? Was the work executed rapidly or might it have evolved slowly over a long period? What skills must the artist have required to produce such a work?

MOOD

Does the work affect you, the viewer, in any way? Does it capture a mood, feeling or emotion which you have already experienced? Does it convey feelings about life and nature? Can you imagine what the artist's feelings might have been while producing the work? Is the work quiet or noisy, soothing or disturbing, happy or sad, relaxing or jarring, etc., in the mood it conveys and the feelings it arouses? Is your mood simply the one of the moment or has the work directly affected you? If the latter, what are the qualities that so affect you? [26]

At a recent GCSE training day, Wigan art and design teachers produced some impressively perceptive writing during a workshop session in which they applied these four categories to original works of their choice on display at the *Drumcroon Education Art Centre*. Recognising the significance of contexts, an important aspect of this workshop was the identification of other works—past and present—which related to the chosen pieces thematically, formally, through use of process or media, or through their evocation of similar moods and atmospheres. This cut dramatically across the convention of there being only 'one particular correct interpretation and meaning.' This attitude can still deter the teacher from adopting *Critical Studies* approaches of course, but it is currently under attack to the extent that those who choose to enter the *Critical Studies* arena now do so at an exciting and challenging time.

The tendency to divorce formal properties from content is being reconsidered. The gender issue is causing both historical re-evaluations and reconsideration of the role of women artists in contemporary society. A 'world view' is developing in contrast to the Eurocentric one which has predominated for so long. Folk and popular art forms are being seen as worthy of greater attention, as are aspects of the crafts and a wide variety of designed and manufactured objects. The boundaries that have traditionally separated these areas from works regarded as 'great' are becoming increasingly blurred in terms of their validity for study.

Compared with some other curriculum areas, levels of debate in art and design are currently of a high order, and it would be a tragedy if the subject were diminished by being shunted into a ten per cent 'arts ghetto' as a consequence of the National Curriculum debate. The *conceptual, productive* and *contextual and critical* domains are applicable. across the whole art, craft and design spectrum. Art and design education is better placed now than it has been for years to reconcile this breadth with the depth of profound experiences—from the most express-ive act to the design-orientated and functional activities—that equally characterise the subject. *Critical Studies* is absolutely essential to this reconciliation. As Marie, a fifth form pupil observed:

> Everybody is influenced by somebody else and if you could just start to formulate your own ideas, just follow the guidelines of somebody else's work and not exactly copy, just understand how they have done it, what they were thinking of and how they put it all together, instead of just doing one simple print of just a figure or something like that—and really go to town on things like that. Just to have the chance to tax your brain. . . . [27].

Notes and References

1   TAYLOR, R. 1986. *Educating for Art: Critical Responses and Development.* London, Longman.
2   NORTHERN EXAMINING ASSOCIATION. 1988. *GCSE Art and Design Syllabuses*, p. 4.
3   SECONDARY EXAMINING COUNCIL WORKING PARTY. 1988. *Art and Design Grade Criteria Report*, pp. 6–7.
4   In these bleak times, the *Drumcroon Education Art Centre*, Wigan, has become a symbol of hope to many art and design educators around the country. It demonstrates how school and gallery-based work can interrelate and the worth—not only for young people but also for the adult community—of organising an exhibition programme in which educational needs are always uppermost. Study of the exhibited works and practical workshops naturally interweave and exhibition themes, processes and values are constantly affirmed through the use of books drawn from the Centre's library, so as to demon-strate to visitors of all ages links across time, places and cultures. Pupils return with friends and relatives at weekends; Drumcroon's young visitors frequently assume the role of teachers. The Loan Collection of original works, over a thousand strong, is available to all schools. Artists and craftspeople both work in the Centre and are resident in schools, as well as contributing to Saturday morning classes. Many of the visitors from around the country have ambitions to create equivalent resources in their own localities, and it is to be hoped that many more young people will thus similarly benefit in the not too distant future.
5   TAYLOR, *ibid*. Note 1, p. 68. See also Taylor, R. 1987. 'Critical Studies and the Drumcroon Experience', *Journal of Art and Design Education* Vol. 6, No. 2.
6   TAYLOR, *ibid*. Note 1, p. 112.
7   TAYLOR, *ibid*. Note 1, p. 226.
8   SEC *ibid*. Note 3, p. 9.
9   TAYLOR, *ibid*. Note 1, p. 227.
10 Based on a recorded conversation between Samantha and Rod Taylor 21.9.84. See TAYLOR; J.A.D.E., *ibid*. Note 5.

11 SEC *ibid.* Note 3, p. 9.
12 TAYLOR, *ibid.* Note 1, p. 165.
13 TAYLOR, R. 1988. *Wigan Schools, Critical Studies and GCSE Art and Design.* Wigan, Drumcroon Occasional Publication, p. 17.
14 BARRETT, M. 1988. 'A Critical Look at Critical Studies'. North West NSEAD Conference, Manchester Polytechnic, 12.3.88.
15 BARRETT, M. 1988. Manchester Cornerhouse Presentation. 18.1.88.
16 READ, H. 1937. *Art and Society.* London, Heinemann, p. 223.
17 TOMLINSON, R. R. 1947. *Children as Artists.* Harmondsworth, King Penguin, p. 27.
18 RICHARDSON, M. 1948. *Art and the Child.* London University Press, p. 23.
19 ROBERTSON, S. 1963. *Rosegarden and Labyrinth.* London, Routledge and Kegan Paul (rep. Gryphon Press, 1982), p. xxix.
20 MARSHALL, S. 1963. *An Experiment in Education.* Cambridge University Press, p. 171.
21 GENTLE, K. 1985. *Children and Art Teaching.* Croom Helm, p. 77.
22 READ, H. 1943. *Education through Art.* London, Faber, p. 298.
23 See, for example, the identification of potential primary sources for Critical Studies in the work of Andrew Mortimer, Chapter 5.
24 BRIGHTON MUSEUM, THE TATE GALLERY, BRIGHTON POLYTECHNIC. 1983. *Museums and Art Galleries in the Teaching of Art and Design.* Course Handbook 1983–4, p. 1.
25 See HUGHES, A. 1981. 'A Place for Art History in the Art and Design Curriculum?', in: *The Pull of the Future.* City of Birmingham Polytechnic.
26 TAYLOR, *ibid.* Note 13, p. 5.
27 TAYLOR, *ibid.* Note 1, p. 45.

Chapter Four

MIKE HILDRED New Ways of Seeing

For a good many years now I have been interested in the idea that young people at all levels of education can bring penetrating intuitions, observations and judgements to bear upon works of art—when their minds are not clouded by the attitudes and opinions of adults. Moreover, while teachers may frequently have agonised over the most appropriate sequence of facts and 'isms' to present to different age groups, we may have overlooked one of the most potent facts of all—namely the silent power of the work of art itself. This chapter looks at some of the background to this thinking and how it found its way into courses for 14-year-old pupils in Scotland; encouraging them to turn normal art room practices into processes of appreciation and stimulating them to employ their own personal vocabulary as critics and connoisseurs, focusing upon the wonderful collections in the museums and galleries of Scotland.

The courses are fully described in a report entitled *New Ways of Seeing* [1], which breaks down the structure of art appreciation into five clearly defined components, four of which lean heavily upon a book by H. Osborne, published in 1970, entitled *The Art of Appreciation* [2]. Osborne shed considerable light upon the process of appreciation by distinguishing four major components to which he gave equal value. He stated that all four needed to be activated before any appreciation process could be fully realised. They comprised *critical activity, history of art, connoisseurship* and *aesthetic experience.*

Clearly, to be useful in schools these traditional areas of art scholarship needed to be democratised for everyday use. However, it was extremely helpful to have such a sharply defined structure. Without one, art teachers are locked into a familiar position of making art history the sole justification for asserting that they teach appreciation. Osborne's categories allow us to approach youngsters with an enriched, more flexible concept. A brief description of them will follow later. For the moment it suffices to say that to his four elements I added a fifth—namely the *production of art and design.*

Subsequently I have tended to put this last element at the top of the list, hoping thereby to dispel a fear that may linger in the minds of some art teachers that we are in an 'either/or' situation; and that a focus upon contexts of appreciation sounds the death-knell of practical work. What is proposed is just the reverse. Practical processes must be an integral part of all this. Taking an example from ceramics, all the manipulative, tactile, creative educational values normally ascribed to youngsters making pots, are now put into a context in which no purely verbal persuasion can so surely give direct insight into what potters do and achieve, nor add so sharp a stimulus and cutting edge to the expression of views about other types of pots, which pots 'work', which are liked, disliked, or liked under certain conditions of use, environment, lighting and so on. Practical and critical processes go hand-in-hand, each informing the other. Importantly, critical attitudes can be turned inwards too.

Though influential in the design of my own courses, Osborne's specialist book on the theory of appreciation was not directed towards art in schools. However, other publications were pointing strongly towards the direction in which educational change in the subject should flow. In *Studies in Art Education*, under the title 'A proper function for art education in the seventies', (1970), E. J. Kern suggested that one of the most important roles for the visual arts in education rested on their acting as models for visual-aesthetic experience in the development of critical skills [3]. As we have seen, critical activity had also been described by Osborne in 1970 as an essential component of appreciation. It took a little while for it to surface as an obligatory element in the new GCSE and Standard Grade (Scotland) examinations.

The same year, in his book *Change in Art Education*, (1970), Dick Field spoke of the need for pupils to learn to see art in a social context and to become responsive, active, creative and courageously discriminating in their attitudes as future consumers [4]. Much that has followed since in education seems to hinge upon growing concern for issues surrounding pupils seen as consumers—not only of the products of art and design but of school curricula and, in the end of course, life itself. More open-ended questions have been seen increasingly as needing to be *asked* by teachers across the curriculum, requiring redeployment of teaching skills in terms of *listening* to what pupils tell them and *recognising* what is said; giving pupils of all ages more practice in expressing and justifying their opinions.

In 1972, John Berger broadcast his series of four programmes on BBC television under the title *Ways of Seeing*—and there was also a Penguin book based on the series [5]. In itself this raises one or two questions which are reflected in the content of my course, with regard to the extent to which different communications media are able to reflect the same message. Although Berger's book was illustrated and was clearly based upon the TV series, nevertheless it was the actual television programmes that left an enduring impression on my mind—and not simply because of Berger's fixating presentation. When all other issues behind his programmes had had time to filter down into the sediments of my mind in the intervening years, one or two influential impressions continued to bob about and shimmer near the surface. One was to do with media reproductions, their massive proliferation in modern times and the ways in which we are presented with, and tend to perceive *facts*.

Now of course, original *artefacts* are facts, and like many of us, Berger was particularly concerned with the effects reproduction processes have upon the role and value of original works of art and how they and the artists who produce them are consequently perceived by the general public. Another buoyant impression left by the programmes, (perhaps because of the discomfort it aroused) was of his calling into question the utterances and interpretations of paintings by experts, in books and in the media generally. There might be more than a suspicion that art teachers were not entirely free of his criticism of art gurus, who unload a lot of mystifying clap-trap about the subject onto audiences who, given encouragement to look and think for themselves, could extract a wealth of pertinent meanings from direct contact with art images—and he used a small group of primary children to demonstrate his point.

Now, I know there have been substantial challenges to Berger's viewpoints in *Ways of Seeing* and, in any case, I was not inclined to go all the way down the path along which his ideas led. Nevertheless, some of the questions he raised just would not seem to go away. Perhaps in the end it boiled down to questions of balance and degree, and I felt that, since traditional practices in school, (my own included), tended to lean heavily towards the historical element in appreciation, it might be worth experimenting a little further in other directions, to see how *little* young people might need to be told about paintings, to still derive satisfaction and qualities of appreciation, from which a natural desire for history might grow.

The opportunity to find out came in 1981, when I was invited to create a pilot course for 14-year-olds that would embody the changes recommended in three reports published in Scotland in 1977. These were the *Pack, Munn* and *Dunning Reports* [6]. They dealt individually with truancy and indiscipline in Scottish schools, proposals for change in the structure of curriculum in the third and fourth year of the Scottish secondary school, and assessment for all. A major outcome of the reports has been the development of the Standard Grade Examination to replace 'O' Grade in Scotland. My own courses have been presented in the evolving context of the new exam.

From a personal point of view the *Pack Report* on truancy and indiscipline seemed fundamental. Under a heading of 'Attitudes and Motivation', it suggested that one part of the problem lay in teachers under-estimating the capacities of their children, that pupils tend to try to match the expectations of their teachers—and too little is asked of many pupils. Whilst these notions were not new to educational research, they took on particular force when given expression in the context of this report. In addition Pack set out a list of desirable objectives for teachers. Among these was the provision of systematic guidance and help for pupils to develop power to make informed choices. The report suggested:

> The decision to establish pupil choice at the centre of curriculum
> design could, we believe, prove to be justified by a growth in the
> involvement of the pupils in their own work, and with that, greater
> interest in it, deeper concern for its purposes, and a stronger drive
> and determination to do well [7].

These sentiments align nicely with the aims and aspirations of my course in practical appreciation, where pupil choice is central to the use of assignment cards, practical work and visits to printing firm and gallery.

So what is the course like? Before describing it, it might be helpful if I mention that in Scotland children move into the secondary sector a year later than in England and Wales, so that 14-year-olds are entering their third year and take the 'O' Grade at the end of the fourth year. The Higher, the equivalent to A-level, is taken one year later and there is a further exam called the Certificate of Sixth Year Studies (CSYS) that can be taken by those staying on into the sixth form.

A little earlier I stated that one objective of my course would be to see how *little* one might need to tell young people about paintings, 'isms' or anything else, at the outset of processes of appreciation. Certainly at third year level there was no difficulty finding youngsters who knew nothing about art history—and cared even less. The same could be said about local galleries and the pictures in them—even the Scottish paintings. And this of course is despite the fact that for Lothian and Edinburgh children a good number of local galleries are National Galleries, with collections that attract enthusiasts from all corners of the globe. But there are many other galleries in Scotland and, in more remote places, castles, with rich collections that also remain relatively neglected by schools in their areas.

14 A 14-year-old 'O' Grade Certificate pupil using an assignment card in the National Gallery of Scotland, Edinburgh. (photo: Hildred, M)

So, on the whole we were approaching fallow ground and it would be a matter of exploring it in the first place through direct contact with images *in schools* which are not normally endowed with original works of art—if we discount pupil works. In addition, and so that appreciation processes could integrate naturally with practical experiences in printing, drawing, painting and photography, the images we would start with would be reproductions—postcard reproductions. The course is intended as an alternative to traditional approaches, whereby chronological art history is presented as a one-way communication of externally selected facts and judgements. At secondary level, this process has often taken the form of slide lectures, or the use of slide packs in isolation from practical work and has been directed largely towards passive candidates for higher qualifications. I wanted to provide a structure that would encourage youngsters to look at images in a variety of ways and for a longer period of time, before expressing their opinions.

15 L S LOWRY *Canals and Factories*, oil on canvas, reproduced by courtesy of Mrs Carol Ann Danes. (photo: Scottish National Gallery of Modern Art, National Galleries of Scotland, Edinburgh)

The written response of a 14-year-old (Scottish third year) pupil:
'Factory chimneys are the highest buildings, belching out smoke.
Children playing in streets.
Industrial setting.
Men walking home from work in factory.
Little tug boats on the canal.
Children playing on canal bank.
Church tower and clock with surrounding trees.
Some buildings brick red. Adds colour to grey picture.
Football pitch being played on.

There are a lot of children in this painting done in very small detail. Most of them are playing in the street or by the canal. The rest of the figures are all men, dressed in dark clothes probably going home from work. There is little vegetation in the painting, as would be expected in an industrial town, however there are a few trees around the church and some grass growing in the foreground. It is a very dull dreary day probably in late spring, judging by the foliage on the trees. Almost all of the painting is devoted to industry and the people who live and work there, the only relief from the tension of industry is the church which has maintained the treat of green trees. I think it is an observed point of view and maybe Lowry experienced the same conditions and maybe lived there.

I think Lowry was trying to show upper class people how the working people lived. I think the picture shows that Lowry has had experience of some sort of conditions in an industrial town. I don't think Lowry is 'keen' on industrial towns he just wants to show a different way of life to the richer folk.

I like the picture. It shows how hard some people find it to live decently. I would not like to live there but I like knowing what it would look and feel like to be in that situation. It makes you feel well off and lucky to be in a better situation than the people in the painting. It does not tell me how it would be to live at a different time but it did tell me how it would be like to live in a different place with a lot less income. You cannot see the clothing very well but it looks dark and made for working in. The children's clothes are not pretty but are worn for playing in. The children would probably have one nice set of clothes for church which we can see in the picture.'

An important feature is the use of postcard reproductions of paintings from the National Galleries in Edinburgh, from Glasgow's Kelvingrove and from the Museum and Art Gallery at Kirkcaldy. The postcards are mounted on assignment sheets which include a structured range of standardised, open-ended questions, suggestions for follow-up activities and a little basic information about the image on the card. Printed facts are limited to things like the name and dates of the artist, the collection in which the original image can be found, the medium, and, very important, the measurements of the original image. By means of a simple measuring exercise to recreate the dimensions printed on the card, pupils can become aware of the wide variety of sizes in original works of art, compared with the deceptive similarity in postcard reproductions. I believe this provides an important foundation to education about the media, whilst contributing a very useful element of preparation in the classroom for eventual contact with original paintings.

I am confident the assignment cards can be adapted to paintings in any public or private collection and eventually I hope to show that they can be applied to wider fields of art and design. However, I deliberately chose to feature painting in the first instance because, in the present climate of accountability in which design processes may more easily keep their place in the sun, I felt it would be a mistake to overlook the educational contribution that drawing and painting can also make, as relatively economical, universal modes for promoting varied ideas, concepts of design, problem-solving, manipulative skill, visual awareness, critical appreciation—and, of course, creativity and the externalising of feeling. Their variety of form and content constitutes an essential part of their function to embody and communicate different ideas. The

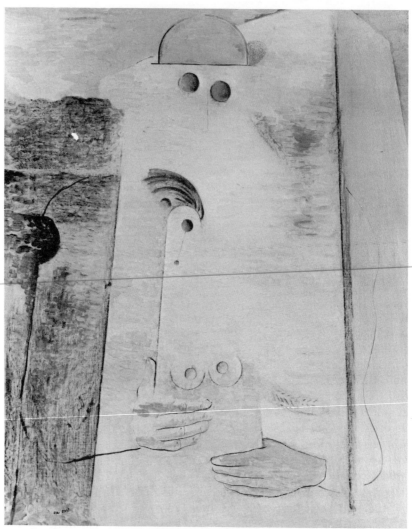

16   MAX ERNST *Grand Amoreux*, oil on canvas, Scottish National Gallery of
Modern Art, National Galleries of Scotland, Edinburgh, © DACS, 1989.

Transcript of a tape-recorded response of a 14-year-old (Scottish third
year) pupil.
'The things I noticed in the picture were the heart, the clouds; the hands,
the arm, the breasts and the different shades of colour in the picture.

This picture is out of the artist's imagination. It shows there are two
people or things in the picture. The big one is the man holding the lady in
his arms. It is during the day, the sky is very colourful. The interesting
objects are in the centre of the picture, with a few lines in other parts. There
are dark colours mixed with light colours. He is trying to draw attention to
the most important parts by drawing black lines.'

same media link both traditional and innovative concepts, and I believe
our children should be educated to appreciate that link. I wanted to
explore the extent to which youngsters can accommodate this variety in
the classroom and how far they are able to extract pertinent meanings
directly from paint images, with the minimum of adult intervention.

The assignment cards constitute initial and continuing stimulus on the course and can be grouped and used in different ways, which I outline in the report. But I regard as fundamental the process whereby pupils are invited to make an open selection from a range of images that includes famous, less famous, and neglected works of art. It means that some may choose to breathe new life and value into well-nigh forgotten works, in company with others who opt to reinforce the famous. Discussion should be a natural outcome of the process. In this approach, critical activity and much else besides, starts with the free choice of image. For the purposes of the course, I adapted Osborne's structure of appreciation to produce the following brief definitions of appropriate components in a close-knit relationship.

Production of art and design: in this context indicates first-hand experience of art/craft/design processes as an important mode of art appreciation. Such a view of practical work may be the most appropriate focus in the education of school children, most of whom will become consumers and, in the professional sense, non-practitioners, once they have left school.

Critical activity: involves comparison, evaluation and judgement. It can be applied by an individual to his or her own products, or it can be directed outwards towards evaluation of the work of others. Any data that the critic deems relevant, may be used in the formation of his judgements. The *informed critic* who makes *balanced judgements* would seem to be a useful model upon which to base objectives of critical activity.

History of art: largely based in schools upon collation and memorising of externally selected facts. Traditionally, these were presented chronologically, in isolation from practical work, with a back-bone of slide lectures in which pupils were expected to take a relatively passive role. Nevertheless, history is important as the source of our definition of art. It provides the context for art activity.

Connoisseurship: a product of individual contemplation, not normally identified as relevant to school art activities. Based primarily upon very close contact with individual objects, 'conversing' with them, letting them 'speak'. Television has popularised the attitudes of the professional connoisseur in fields as varied as sport and science, antiques, and wildlife, through the personalities of programme presenters like Arthur Negus, David Attenborough and a wide range of sports commentators. However, many young folk, including characters who would generally earn low ratings for artistic sensitivity in class, can demonstrate well-developed capacities for the fine discriminations of the connoisseur when they come to discuss among themselves successful patterns of play in a football match or the latest innovations in teenage fashion, transport or communication. It remains to be seen how far these capacities can be harnessed and developed in the art room.

Aesthetic experience: involves intuitive, individual, sensual enjoyment and an attitude of particular attention to current experience—noticing that you are noticing . . . There are two main sources for triggering aesthetic experience: (i) natural objects, phenomena, and environments; and (ii) man-made objects and environments, including a wide range of artefacts which have been deliberately made to evoke aesthetic responses. For example, paintings viewed as objects feature in the latter category, as does the experience of making paintings.

From this view, any effective programme based upon critical appreciation in schools needs to blend experiences from the above elements and grade them according to the capacities of the particular children for whom they are intended. The basic format of the course is essentially flexible and versions have been successfully adapted for the primary school. However, the courses described in the report are directed towards Scottish secondary pupils in their third and fourth years, aged 14 to 16+.

The initial course started at a school in Lothian Region in 1981 and has been continuously run with mixed-ability youngsters since then in the evolving context of the new Standard Grade Examination. In the same context, another strand of the course has been in continuous operation for five years, with classes of pupils with learning difficulties, in Fife. Yet another variation has taken the form of short modules in otherwise normal 'O' Grade Certificate courses for two classes during one year at another school in Lothian Region.

The course blends practical art activities and simple photographic processes, with the use of assignment cards, based on postcard reproductions of paintings and prints from Scottish galleries and museums. The general nature of the course, its visits and its focus upon paintings and media reproductions, means that core practical work tends to be in the area of printing, drawing, painting, photography and graphic design. Nevertheless, it is confidently suggested that sculpture and other products of three-dimensional design can be easily integrated into the format—where the objects have been reproduced as two-dimensional images, which can be similarly used to point up anomalies between original objects of art and design and reproductions.

Postcard images are presented individually on an assignment-sheet, which includes standardised instructions, questions and information, designed to stimulate the desired learning through the pupil's own initiative as much as possible. The workcards crop up at all sorts of different times in the course, like lenses through which to view practical work, the printing, drawing, etc., and also the visits. It's a matter of judgement on the part of teachers running the project whether class responses are best recorded by pupils in writing, or on tape or film or a combination of all three. This also goes for visits to galleries and printing firms.

Thanks to the help of Mr David Garland, Head of Art Department at Lasswade High School (the first school to pilot the course), it was possible to arrange class visits to a printing company in Musselburgh which had printed many of the postcard reproductions used by the National Galleries in Edinburgh. This was ideal, because it made available almost as clear a link-up as one is likely to get between simple

17 14-year-old pupils made collages, photographed them, and
subsequently compared the original and its monochrome reproduction.
Duncan Lyall wrote of his work:
'I like the picture better than the photograph because of the colour and the
detail is not so well seen in the photograph. The picture and the photo
would have been better if all the eyes had blended together. The picture is
meant to resemble the eyes of the world looking at the Royal Family ...'
(photo: Hildred, M)

processes in the classroom, postcard reproductions used as visual aids,
the commercial printers of the postcards, and galleries that house original
art from which the postcards were produced. The main objective is to
witness the mass production of printed images and relate it to activities
in the classroom.

18   Pamela Murdoch:
'I like the photograph because you can't see where the head, legs and arms join on to the hamburger, and it looks more unusual; but also I like the collage because it is colourful and the sky in the background looks more effective.'
(photo: Hildred, M)

One glance at the sheer range of imagery and ideas embodied in the cards immediately illustrates the local art resources can become windows on the ideas of the world. Within that world local imagery and local ideas are shown, literally, to have their place. How important that place is should become a matter of judgement by the pupils themselves. The postcards are cheap and convenient and help to tie together the many

19 Moria Sheridan:
'Between the collage and the photograph I prefer the photograph because
the collage does not actually look as though it was meant to be because you
can see the joins and the colours don't blend ... Although I prefer the
photograph I wish that maybe the red lips and the cherries could be shown
in their colours instead of black, also the eyeballs on the cherries can hardly
be seen.'
(photo: Hildred, M)

different aspects of the course. The report gives detailed descriptions of
their use as part of the rationale and in the accounts of the teachers
involved. But whatever form the course takes in different schools, it is
intended as a *stimulus for pupils to gain practice in making and justifying
their own aesthetic judgements*.

With regard to critical activity, we must not forget how unfamiliar this
area will be to many of our youngsters. Teachers may have to make a
conscious effort to hold back their own opinions until pupils have gained
confidence and recognised that we really do want to know what they
think. Although they will be encouraged to integrate the use of visual

concepts and terminology with their own personal vocabulary, many will be clumsy in their early attempts. They will need patience, they will need help, and they will need practice, for, like other activities in art and design, expressing opinions takes practice too. It is intended that this course will provide substantial alternatives to the purely merce-nary/acquisitive approach to paintings. Processes of critical activity and practical appreciation lie at its heart, therefore a number of predominant learning outcomes can be expressed in the following way: as a result of the course, pupils should:

1   give evidence of experience and confidence in exercising autonomous choices and preferences relative to a wide spectrum of art and design;

2   be confident in expressing opinions and justifying them relative to a wide range of art and design;

3   be able to show evidence of weighing and balancing various factors in the process of critical activity before coming to judgement;

4   be able to express opinions in group discussions and be tolerant of alternative points of view;

5   be able to apply balanced critical attitudes to the production and evaluation of their own artefacts;

6   be evidently aware of connections between traditional and innovative forms in art and design;

7   be able to demonstrate more varied skills in appraising original arte-facts and reproductions than youngsters who have not yet been on such a course;

8   be more tolerant and resourceful in appraising unfamiliar imagery;

9   demonstrate awareness of differences between original artefacts and media representations;

10   know and be able to relate more things about paintings and other artefacts in local museums and galleries and about the galleries them-selves, than their counterparts on other courses;

11   have accumulated evidence of experience in integrated practical processes such as drawing, designing, painting, printing and photog-raphy, both for normal benefits ascribed to first-hand productive ex-perience in art and design and as stimuli for appreciation and critical activity;

12   be aware of common threads of process, investigation, context, design, production, evaluation, recording and media representation underlying fine art, expressive, craft and design processes.

Conclusion

The best way to get a sense of how well pupils responded to the course is to read the report *New Ways of Seeing* and see the video of the same title [8]. It contains detailed course outlines, learning outcomes, a sample assignment card and examples of the practical and critical work of pupils. It also presents the evaluations of five different teachers which deserve to be read in full. Results have been very highly encouraging. All the teachers confirm that the cards work extremely well and there are many examples of pupils identifying very closely with pictures of their choice, making them 'their own' paintings and demonstrating a marked increase in commitment to practical work, visits and critical activity.

The outline of the course contains many suggestions for appropriate art activities, some of which were never tried at all. But one thing that all the teachers did and seemed to find useful was to get their classes to enlarge and copy a chosen image, or work in the same style as their chosen artist at least once. There were signs that this had positive benefit for subsequent paintings in the pupil's own style.

Another achievement of the course on a fairly large scale has been to bring about the opportunity for youngsters to visit a gallery for the first time. One of the teachers tells us that 90 per cent of his three consecutive groups had never been to a gallery before. Something like this proportion seemed true for all classes helping with this experiment. The visit did not need to be long. The main purpose of the first visit was to find the favourite painting, compare it with the postcard and maybe see one or two more. Most children purchased more postcards for themselves. Another teacher tells us 'the class adopted the same method they had used in class—not the usual glance—something much more discerning.'

Encouraging awareness of the effects of media reproduction upon original artefacts has been a natural outcome of the structure of the course and of the assignment cards. In my view it symbolises the significant role for art and design in education about the media. There is a real danger that we undervalue the debt modern media owe to the arts of earlier times. The power of the patron to influence the message is as old as time itself, affecting the products of both pre- and post-camera communications media. The modern leaning towards non-verbal communications is a rekindling of our inheritance from the vastness of pre-industrial history. This is the fertile territory that modern media-manipulators busily exploit. I believe it is a proper concern for educators in art and design.

Whatever the outcome for the new examinations, I hope that courses in critical appreciation will survive and grow. Mine was devised originally to attend to a gap in the overall curriculum of art and design. It is flexible and adaptable. One of its most striking successes has been with classes with learning difficulties. Its requirements in terms of new resources can be quite modest. Its greatest asset lies in the largely untapped human resources of our pupils. As one of the teachers so aptly tells us, 'the latent material is there to be awakened.'

Notes and References

1 HILDRED, M. *et al.* 1986. *New Ways of Seeing*. Edinburgh, Moray House College of Education.
2 OSBORNE, H. 1970. *The Art of Appreciation*. Oxford, Oxford University Press.
3 KERN, E. J. *op. cit.*, Vol. 12, No. 1, 1970.
4 FIELD, D. *op. cit.*, London, Routledge and Kegan Paul, 1970.
5 BERGER, J. 1972. *Ways of Seeing*. Harmondsworth, Penguin/BBC.

6 DUNNING, J. 1977. *Assessment for All*. Edinburgh, Scottish Education Department (report of the Committee to Review Assessment in the 3rd and 4th years of Secondary Education in Scotland).
MUNN, J. 1977. *The Structure of the Curriculum in the Third and Fourth Years of Scottish Secondary Schools*. Edinburgh, HMSO/Scottish Education Department.
PACK, D. C. 1977. *Truancy and Indiscipline in Schools in Scotland*. Edinburgh, Scottish Education Department (report of a Committee of Inquiry appointed by the Secretary of State for Scotland).
7 PACK, *op. cit.* (Note 6).
8 Available from Moray House College of Education, Holyrood Road, EDINBURGH EH8 8AQ

Chapter Five

ANDREW MORTIMER Approaches to the Teaching of Critical Studies

The case for the inclusion of *Critical Studies* in art education is now well established. It can be traced in philosophical and curricular terms for over half a century, from John Dewey's seminal *Art as Experience* (1934) through the work of Allison, Broudy, Eisner, Feldman, Field, Read, Reid, Ross, Witkin, and many others in Britain and the USA. The strength and validity of this collective argument are demonstrated in many ways. It has undoubtedly effected reform in art and design public examination syllabuses, especially the new GCSE; it influenced the former Schools Council to contribute funds to the *Critical Studies in Art Education* project (1981–84); and it has clearly left its mark on the Gulbenkian report *The Arts in Schools* (1982).

In the classroom, however, the conversion of theory into practice does not appear to have been so consistent. The development of teaching strategies seems, at worst, non-existent, and at best patchy in terms of quality, age-range provision, and geographical spread. This is largely dependent on such factors as initial teacher training or retraining; school and Local Education Authority resources; and support from LEA advisory staff, as well as other agencies, including museums, galleries and Regional Arts Associations. On the credit side, certain teacher educational establishments and LEAs are in the forefront of change, and there has been an increased involvement of the Arts Council of Great Britain and the Crafts Council, largely implemented through the RAAs. In addition, some museums and galleries have developed new ways of working that have encouraged close pedagogical links with schools. There has been enough tangible progress to suggest a model of the principal approaches to teaching *Critical Studies* and to examine some of these in terms of their benefits and pitfalls. These methods are numerous, of course, but they may be discussed under two main headings: *The use of primary sources* and *The use of secondary sources*.

1. The use of primary sources

Primary sources are likely to be more stimulating than secondary, however well produced or imaginatively selected the latter might be. It would seem unlikely that a pupil could experience what David Hargreaves has called a 'conversive traumatic experience' [1], or what Rod Taylor prefers to call 'the illuminating experience' [2], from a reproduction or a secondary source. Evidence collected by these two authors would suggest that awareness of scale, medium and detail, as well as notions of 'presence' or 'occasion', are all extremely important features of a heightened experience of art. This is certainly supported by the

57

20   THÉODORE GÉRICAULT
The Raft of the Medusa,
1819, oil on canvas 193 ×
282"; Louvre, Paris.

following statement by one of my 13-year-old pupils. She tells of her reaction to Théodore Géricault's *The Raft of the Medusa*, which she had studied in reproduction and then in a television programme before persuading her parents to take her to Paris to see the original.

From the TV programme I learnt an enormous amount of history and background information about the artist and the painting. . . . This helped me to understand the painting. But the film didn't do the picture justice. The painting was unexplainable. It covered a space bigger than the end wall of the assembly hall . . . it caught my eye immediately, the moment I walked into the room I was mesmerised. . . . What I knew in theory could now be put into practice, just sitting imagining the pain and hunger the survivors were suffering. My imagination was running loose about how they got into that situation in the first place and what would become of them. As my eyes scanned every inch of the picture, I spotted something that wouldn't be visible at first sight. It was a ship in the background of the painting. Suddenly the painting just fell into place. I now knew what the people on the raft were vigorously waving at.

This tiny dot on the horizon of the picture would be unknown to thousands of people who spend only seconds glancing at the figures in the painting.

This account highlights precisely the problem of the use of secondary sources ('the film didn't do the picture justice'), and outlines a process of growing empathetic understanding, from initial intellectual comprehension, to emotional involvement, by way of careful scrutiny of the actual object.

The use of original art work seen in museums, galleries and exhibitions

Parallel movements over the past twenty years, focusing on this sort of educational experience, have been pressurising museums and galleries to reconsider their function. The first was a feeling among several art historians, from whose ranks curators were usually drawn, that there were

shortcomings in academic art history. Much of it [had] moved away from what ordinary people see and think [3].

This debate recommended

the abolition of the demarcation line between some sort of aesthetic appreciation and the cognitive corpus of art history [4].

Further, it pointed to the fact that museums and galleries

have tended to estrange the works they bring together from their original functions [5].

For the art teacher the implications of these radical notions offered an alternative to the academic, chronologically-bound body of knowledge which traditionally governed the approach to art history in schools. It also called into question the divisions between 'high' and 'low' culture, and attacked the cult of the end product—the framed masterpiece.

A second important pressure for change came from curatorial staff themselves [6]. They sought a better balance between the priority of preservation and the educational role of museums and galleries. This, in turn, has led to the appointment of staff—education officers, and seconded teachers to work in and with galleries—to promote more imaginative links between exhibitions and schools' curricula. As Katy Macleod notes in Chapter 8, galleries can now offer schools opportunities to study original works of art carefully, to meet visiting artists, and to hold workshops where teachers and pupils may work together. This in turn provides a range of new perspectives on art, views of different artistic techniques and skills, and also the notion that art history is going on at the present moment, and is therefore a continuum.

Many teachers, trainers, education authorities and museums have recognised the need for and potential value of links between schools and galleries [7]. Australian research into school excursions has shown that where 'active experiences' are incorporated into visits, greater learning takes place [8]. Many types of participatory exhibitions currently offered to school parties could be considered experiences of this sort—as opposed to the simple 'passive' visit to a gallery. In Sweden, research has also shown that there is a strong correlation between the benefits gained from exhibitions and the level of the visitor's own creative activity [9]. Nevertheless, it is important that further, more detailed research into the effectiveness of school/gallery links be carried out to help teachers and curators alike.

The use of original art work on loan to a school

Loan collections of original art works which can be borrowed and used by schools can reduce the need for lengthy and expensive out-of-school trips, and provide teachers with longer and more frequent opportunities to relate relevant objects to their pupils' own practical work. Many LEAs have built up such collections. In Chapter 7 John Bowden describes a project centred on the *Original Works of Art Collection* of the School Museum and Resource Service operated by a consortium of Yorkshire Education Authorities. This is a resource of great value, but there appears to have been little research in this country into what should constitute the content of such collections or their most effective use. It now seems appropriate to consider these questions, as well as syllabus content in *Critical Studies* education as a whole. It would be appropriate, for example, to ask whether they contain a useful balance of items representing the work of craftspeople as well as 'fine' artists, and of women as well as men; whether they are culturally wide-ranging and not Euro-centric or parochial; and include both established and avant-garde or experimental examples of art and design. It would also seem sensible to engage art teachers themselves in the selection procedures for such a potentially useful teaching aid. This would certainly increase the likelihood that it could be used by all phases of education, and be more directly relevant to teacher and pupil needs.

There is also a case to be made for choosing pictures and art objects, for classroom use, with regard to research of educational psychologists into the relationships between pupils' personalities (e.g. introvert/extrovert; field dependent/field independent, etc.) and their aesthetic preferences [10]. Teachers need to be aware of pupil responses to both making and looking at art in the light of such findings, in order to maximise the chance of selecting work with the broadest appeal [11]. Whatever original work teachers borrow, their purpose in showing it to pupils needs to be clearly defined. Questions need to be asked about whether exhibiting such examples is intended to stimulate ideas, study techniques, encourage a better understanding of the creative process or of what artists make, or a combination of these aspects [12].

The use of visits and residencies by practising professional artists and craftspeople

Both the Arts Council and the Crafts Council have, over the past ten years or so, encouraged artists and craftspeople to take part in schemes in which they talk about their work, demonstrate, or simply work on their own projects in the context of a school. The administration of such schemes has mostly been devolved to the various RAAs in co-operation with LEAs. The purpose of this approach has been defined by Pat van Pelt, a former Art Education Officer at the Arts Council:

A school environment, by its very nature, tends to be insular and isolated. All we can do to enrich and enlarge this world is therefore vital. An artist brings to the school a wealth of new experiences from which s/he selects, records, examines, rejects, reassesses, codes and decodes. To be witness, even in part, to this process, both stimulates enquiry and heightens perception [13].

Statements about the potential benefits of such placements abound [14], and clearly their development is central to any notion of *Critical Studies* because they can:

offer a unique opportunity for increasing understanding by pupils of the nature of the creative practice, coupled with the values, aspirations and lifestyles of people who live by their creative skills. Face to face contact with experienced professionals offers a challenge to pupils' own art work and offers staff, too, an exchange of fresh ideas and information [15].

A feature of any such scheme is what might be termed the 'style' of the placement [16]. This might be overtly 'instructional', if the visiting artist is introducing new skills, or 'inspirational' when, perhaps by doing his or her own work, the visitor acts as a catalyst, in terms of ideas and/or techniques, for an already 'semi-skilled' group of pupils. Other

21 Charcoal drawing by a 15-year-old girl. Her visit to a practising artist's studio led to a marked development of technique in her own work.
(photo: Mortimer, A)

aspects of the 'style' might include consideration of the length of placement in school; the amount of time set aside for the artist's own work; the amount of direct pupil contact; the range of pupils to be helped; the commissioning of work for the school; associated exhibitions; and so forth. These and other organisational factors require careful planning prior to setting up a scheme. Ground rules concerning function, roles and procedures need to be established for the benefit of all concerned and, whenever possible, forms of evaluation built in.

The use of statements made by artists about their work

Closely linked to the use of artists and craftspeople in schools is the approach which examines the development of ideas and the creative process through consideration of artists' verbal accounts of their work. Authentic supporting statements can be of great importance and considerable help in increasing pupil understanding—in the same way that sketches or preliminary studies might be. The thoughts of an artist, living or dead, can be discovered from letters, diaries, journals, manifestos and other sources. Such statements can also focus attention onto issues like purpose and style in art. For example:

> When you go out to paint, try to forget what objects you have before you—a tree, a house, a field or whatever. Merely think, here is a little square of blue, here is an oblong of pink, here is a streak of yellow, and paint it just as it looks to you, the exact colour and shape. (Monet, as reported by Lilla Cabot Perry in 1927.)

or

> . . . instead of trying to reproduce exactly what I see before my eyes, I use colour more arbitrarily, in order to express myself forcibly. (van Gogh, letter to Theo, 1888.)

or

> Art is the opposite of nature. A work of art can come only from the interior of man. (Munch, quoted in Langaard and Revold, 1963.)

Read in conjunction with analyses of the actual art works themselves (or even reproductions), such comments clarify or challenge critical judgements.

It is also possible, through such evidence, to explore changes and developments in style within individual artists' work. For example, two of van Gogh's letters help explain a shift in his thinking that is clearly perceptible in the paintings themselves.

> And in a picture I want to say something comforting, as music is comforting.

and

> I have tried to express the terrible passions of humanity by means of red and green. (van Gogh, letters to Theo, 1888.)

Such an approach, with carefully-selected examples, can not only increase pupil awareness of the work of others, but can raise questions about the purpose and methods of their own work. Parts of the following statement by Matisse might easily be paraphrased and understood by

62

pupils of primary school age and equated with their own work.

> The chief aim of colour should be to serve expression as well as possible. I put down my colours without a preconceived plan. . . . What I dream of is an art of balance, of purity and serenity, devoid of troubling or depressing subject matter . . . something like a good armchair in which to rest from physical fatigue. (Matisse, *Notes of a Painter*, 1908.)

Older pupils would be capable of seeing connections and differences between this statement, Matisse's actual paintings, and the ideas of Jackson Pollock as expressed thus:

> I don't work from drawings or colour sketches. My painting is direct. . . . I want to express my feelings rather than illustrate them. (From the artist's narration for the film *Jackson Pollock*, 1951, by Hans Namuth and Paul Falkenberg.)

The use of pupils' and teachers' own art work

In the four preceding examples of approaches to *Critical Studies*, the notion of extending the pupils' art experiences beyond the classroom has been paramount. But such strategies should not lead teachers to overlook the most 'economical' source for developing critical aesthetic awareness—the practical work of the pupils themselves and, whenever possible, that of teachers. If pupils are to be helped to develop self-confidence in their expression of ideas through and about art and design, it would seem sensible to start the process within the 'shelter' of their own or peer-group work. Practice of this through oral or written statements might take the form of short critiques, like these by 11- and 12-year-olds in my school:

> I like the sewing machine picture, because it looks like ivory with its fancy pattern. Also, the person who done it must have looked at every detail, including the cogs which are operating the machine. The shadow is black with tints of blue. The person used pastels which look quite effective. The person has also used shading to give it a three-dimensional shape.

and

> I like this picture. The wall in the foreground has been pastelled in shades of green, red, brown, white and black. The sky is white with black, so the field in the foreground looks bleak and empty except for the hut which looks desolate. (Cumbria Education Authority, 1986.)

David Hargreaves has explained what happens when pupils have little experience of looking at art objects in any serious way:

> They were not used to forming and then expressing judgements about them and were nervous of so doing; and most of all they lacked a working vocabulary in which to talk openly about their reactions, beyond the level of 'I like that' or 'I don't like that' [17].

Despite the fact that language skills are seen as foreign to the domain of the art room by some teachers [18], there is a growing awareness that an extended vocabulary is an essential corollary to *Critical Studies*. Brian

Allison has provided a summary review of recent literature specifically on the use of language in relation to *Critical Studies* and it reveals a growing body of evidence suggesting that conceptual understanding of art is clearly linked to the development of language skills [19].

The teacher's own work, discussed with pupils, is another useful way into establishing critical confidence. Malcolm Ross has defined a sensitive, practising art teacher as one who draws his or her pupils into the area they too inhabit [20]. Research involving the psychological testing of art students suggests that:

> Art is seen as an experience and experience cannot be taught. It can, however, be facilitated by an environment that is both free and stimulating and by people whose sole involvement is with the experience of art [21].

In his book *The Nature of Workmanship* [22] David Pye puts forward the notion of 'workmanship of risk', which involves the possibility of failure. The teacher/artist is undoubtedly the best person to make children aware of, and share, this aspect of the creative process.

It would be an interesting and worthwhile experiment if LEAs were to recognise the significance of such ideas and allow sabbatical time for art teachers to pursue their own work within the structure of their professional development. Nor should the notion of the teacher's own work necessarily be restricted to actual art making—a sensitive, practising art teacher simply means one with a continuing and demonstrable commitment to, and curiosity about, art, its function, and its practice in society.

2. The use of secondary sources

No general national picture exists of the current use of primary sources in *Critical Studies* methodology. If a recent survey of one LEA is typical, however, it would appear that such approaches are the exceptions rather than the rule. On the other hand, the use of secondary source materials like reproductions has been a fairly standard practice for many years. Most art teachers keep selections which they use to enhance their teaching. There is evidence that such collections of books, prints, postcards and slides are usually provided from the teacher's own resources rather than from school capitation [23]. Little need be said about the general use of such material, but it is perhaps worth examining two related issues.

The use of mass-produced images of art work

Many of the examples of classroom practice written about recently [24] use reproductions (especially postcards) as sources for copies, pastiches or borrowings, or else they employ them in crash-courses in art appreciation. The dangers inherent in either of these methods are often overlooked in trying to graft a *Critical Studies* component onto an existing art syllabus. There are certainly no guarantees that by simply copying, enlarging, borrowing from, or imagining 'what might happen next' in a narrative painting, children will acquire an enriched understanding of either a particular artist's work, or its relevance to themselves. What often appears to happen is that the teacher simply replaces one set of images to be copied (frequently selected from magazine colour supplements) with another set culled from 'fine art'. There is little doubt that such work can

> enliven the content of the work of younger children—it can encourage older children towards a more demanding use of such qualities of colour, pigment, tone, surface and space that illustrate many of the works . . . studied [25].

But it can also be restrictive if not used carefully—restrictive in terms of a teacher-dictated choice of image; restrictive in terms of offering only two-dimensional experiences; restrictive in terms of limiting pupils' expressive responses to second-hand styles.

Similarly, if a pupil's critical response is in a verbal form it might well show an

> apt and refreshing analysis [that] has a quality that is unlikely to spring from the adult mind [26].

But *Critical Studies* should not stop here. The teacher must enable the pupil to move on

> towards something more discriminating, finer, richer, fuller, more complex [27].

Most importantly this increased or improved knowledge or understanding must relate the experience to a pupil's own expressive practical work. Secondary source materials should not merely be another stimulus for sterile art exercises.

The use of supporting background material to place art work into a context

All art has a function somewhere on the continuum between the publicly utilitarian and the privately expressive. All art is produced in a cultural or social context. The critical study of art should, therefore, help explain the purposes of art and offer potential models for the pupil's own work. If it fails to do this, a child's contact with artists remains ill-informed. There are many useful, but often neglected, ways of placing art objects or artists into context. These include the study of information (for example, written or filmed) that enhances an understanding of the historical or environmental conditions in which the work was made; reconstructions of the artist's life or social milieu; experimentation with materials or methods associated with the artist; and visiting the site(s) of production, from specific landscapes to actual studios.

General background documentary information or reconstruction of this sort can be a key to capturing a pupil's initial interest, and provide a platform from which a more sustained and informed study might be undertaken. It can also help link art with other curriculum areas (including history, English and other literatures, geography, science, etc.) [28]. The main pitfalls that affect the use of such materials are either that they become a total substitute for primary sources, or that they tend to be used in self-contained packages, rather than as stimuli for more extended study'. . . . . .

Few primary or secondary school teachers will have access to an extensive range of supplementary *Critical Studies* teaching aids. Even where an LEA has established a resource centre, not all its teachers will feel confident or committed enough to use it fully. Further research, evaluation, in-service training and funding are urgently required if *Critical Studies* is to play its full part in education. But whichever strategies are available to individual teachers, the first need is to establish the philosophical or theoretical base which underlies and informs practice. Without this, *Critical Studies* tends to become confused with more traditional notions of art history or art appreciation. These discrete disciplines, like the practical act of making art itself, are neither adequate nor appropriate ways of providing, *on their own*, a *complete* education in or through art. *Critical Studies* should provide for the integration of some of the principal elements of art history, art appreciation, and art criticism with the creative work children do in school. *Critical Studies is therefore an essential adjunct to the pupils' practical work: sometimes it may lead to it, sometimes stem from it* [29]. Some examples of methods used with 13 to 15-year-old pupils may illustrate this precept.

A group of mixed ability visited a local printmaker's studio, where they saw how one artist's ideas were worked through into printed images. They subsequently visited an exhibition of his work, which reinforced the original experience by offering a wider range of examples. For some pupils the benefits of such contact led to marked improvements in the techniques of their own work; while for others it opened up possibilities of themes that were either 'too close' for them to have seen, or which they had not previously considered 'appropriate' for art.

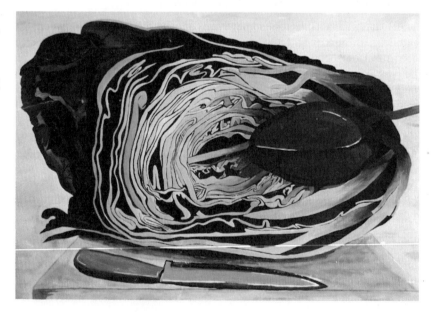

22   *The Heart of the Cabbage,* painting by a 14-year-old girl. Part of a study of Surrealism and its relationship to advertising, this exhibited original and imaginative thought where little had been shown before. (photo: Mortimer, A)

Changed attitudes towards what might constitute 'art' led another group to a study of contemporary advertising. They then undertook an examination of the ideas and styles of Surrealism that appeared to influence many contemporary television commercials. This further extended this group's ideas of what might be defined as 'beautiful' in art. Might it be the bizarre, the surprising or the shocking? Might it result from

> the chance encounter of a sewing machine and an umbrella on a dissecting table? (Ducasse, in *Chants de Maldoror*, Paris 1868–74.)

The pupils' own practical work subsequently explored the theme of making a picture that brought together two or more different images into a new combination. The results were well researched and often startling or amusing. They were rarely parodies, but showed a wealth of original and imaginative thought, where little had been shown before.

Another example started with discussion among 13-year-olds about the capsising and sinking of a pop-singer's yacht in 1986. The group had watched television news about this disaster at sea, and were clearly concerned and moved by the event [30]. At first discussion focused on the way such tragedies were covered by the media—dramatic photographs, unusual camera angles, dangers of seagoing, etc. This led naturally into an examination in books and slides of the work of Turner,

23, 24, 25   *Disaster at Sea* paintings by 13-year-old pupils. Work produced as a result of studying contemporary news events, poetry and other paintings on this theme. GÉRICAULT'S *The Raft of the Medusa* 'seen from a rescuing helicopter'; a historical perspective; and a modern equivalent. (photo: Mortimer, A)

and of how he conveyed the 'news' and drama of his shipwrecks. It was also supported by pupils watching a television programme reconstructing the life of Géricault and the events that led up to his painting of *The Raft of the Medusa*. As a result of consultation between art teacher and colleagues in the history and English departments, the pupils were at the same time studying nineteenth century documentation of disasters at sea, including work like Gerard Manley Hopkins' poem *The Wreck of the Deutschland*. I began this chapter with the poignant example of one pupil's reaction. There was also a generally heightened awareness of aesthetic needs on the part of other pupils, leading to their own paintings of disasters at sea—some contemporary, some specific, some historical.

In all these projects, the *Critical Studies* approach provided a catalyst for art work that was neither copy nor pastiche. The children's work was both original and of high quality because of their extended perceptions of the potential functions and processes of art. Although most work in these examples was narrative, this methodology has an important application to all art work. Such an emphasis prepares pupils for much contemporary art, where concept outweighs outcome; or where conventional art historical analysis fails to come to terms with non-imagist events or non-European traditions; or where art appreciation schemes flounder among subjective value judgements.

Notes and References

1 HARGREAVES, D. 1983. The Teaching of Art and the Art of Teaching, in: HAMMERSLEY, M. and HARGREAVES A. *Curriculum Practice: Some Sociological Case Studies*. London.

2 TAYLOR, R. 1982. *The Illuminating Experience*. Wigan, Critical Studies in Art Education Project Occasional Publication No. 2. See also TAYLOR, R. 1986. *Educating for Art*. London, Longman.

3 STEER, J. 1984. Style and Meaning, in: DYSON, A. (ed) *Prospects for Art and Design History in Schools*. Conference report, V & A Museum, November 1983 University of London Institute of Education.

4 ROUVE, S. 1973. Teaching Art History: a Methodological Reappraisal, in: FIELD, D. and J. NEWICK *The Study of Education and Art*. London, pp. 187–210.

5 MALRAUX, A. 1954. *The Voices of Silence*. New ed 1974, London.

6 See MARCOUSÉ, R. 1961. *The Listening Eye*. London, HMSO. See also HOOPER-GREENHILL, E. 1984. *Art Gallery Audiences and Class Constraints*. Conference paper, Art Gallery and Museum Association Conference, V & A Museum, London.

7 See KELSALL, R. 1983. Towards Critical Study in the Primary School, *Journal of Art and Design Education* Vol. 2, No. 1. See also STEER; *ibid*. Note 3. See also McCORMACK, P. (ed). 1985. *Museums and Art Galleries in the Teaching of Art and Design*. Brighton Polytechnic, Centre for Art and Design Teacher Education.

8 MACKENZIE, A. A. and R. T. WHITE. 1982. Fieldwork in Geography and Long Term Memory Structures, in: WHITE, R. T., Research and the End of Schools as we know them, *Australian Journal of Education* Vol. 28, No. 1.

9 ARNELL, V. *et al*. 1976. *Going to Exhibitions*. Stockholm.

10 See RIDING, R. J. and R. D. PEARSON. 1981. The Relationship between the Personality Dimensions of Extroversion and Field Independence and Art Performance in 13 Year Old Children, *Education Review* Vol. 33, No. 3.

11 See DYSON, A. 1986. The Three-Card Trick: the Reading of Images by Young Children, *Journal of Art and Design Education* Vol. 5, Nos 1, 2.

12 A rather exotic use is illustrated in NATIONAL ASSOCIATION of ART ADVISERS. 1984. *Using Pictures with Children*. Harrogate. Pupils 'play' a Paolozzi print with musical instruments.

13 VAN PELT, P. 1982. in: *5 Artists in Schools*. Calderdale Museums Service and Yorkshire Arts.

14 ROODHOUSE, S: *ibid*. See also various authors. 1983. *Artists Newsletter*, September. See also LATHAM, G. 1983. Artist in Residence at Drumcroon: an Educational Experience, *Journal of Art and Design Education* Vol. 2, No. 1.

15 WEST MIDLANDS ARTS. 1984. *Placements in Schools, Art and Craft*.

16 MORTIMER, A. 1985. *The Concepts and Practice of Teaching Critical Studies in Art Education*. Unpublished Report; Cumbria Education Authority.

17 *Ibid*. Note 1.

18 See ALP, W. 1982. Who has the Books and Why?, in: BENNETT, N and E O'HARE (eds) *The Cost and Use of Books in Cumbrian Secondary Schools*. University of Lancaster, Centre for Educational Research and Development.

19 ALLISON, B. 1988. Art in Context, *Journal of Art and Design Education* Vol. 7, No. 2, 1988.

20 ROSS, M. 1978. *The Creative Arts*. London, Chap 3.

21 BARRON, F. 1974. *Artists in the Making*. New York.

22 PYE, D. 1968. *The Nature and Art of Workmanship*. Cambridge.

23 *Ibid*. Note 16.

24 See CLEMENT, R. 1984. *The Real Thing*. Devon LEA. See also HILDRED, M. 1986. *New Ways of Seeing*. Edinburgh.

25 CLEMENT; *ibid*. Note 24.

26 HILDRED; *ibid*. Note 24.

27 REID, L. A. 1973. Knowledge, Aesthetic Insight and Education, *Proceedings of the Philosophy of Education Society of Great Britain* Vol. 7.

28 Such materials include the whole range of books about the lives and works of individual artists or groups of artists, as well as the many film monographs obtainable from the British Film Institute, the Arts Council and other agencies. Appropriate extracts (for various ages and ability ranges) could be used from television series such as John Berger's *New Ways of Seeing* (BBC, 1973); *5 Revolutionary Artists* (ATV, 1972); *Nineteenth Century Artists and Models* (BBC/RM Arts, 1985); programmes in the Open University Foundation Course in Art; and even full-length feature films such as *Lust for Life* (a romaticised but reasonably accurate account of the life of van Gogh); *La Kermesse Héroique* (with its insights into how a seventeenth century Dutch artist worked and its scenes inspired by Velazquez, Breughel, Hals, etc.); or *Paris—La Belle Époque* (a collection of documentary films which sets the late work of Renoir, Monet and Rodin into the context of that of younger artists like Picasso, Matisse and Chagall).

29 MORTIMER, A. 1986. in: NATIONAL ASSOCIATION FOR EDUCATION IN THE ARTS *Agenda for the Arts*. University of London Institute of Education, Take-Up Series No. 3.

30 Simon le Bon's yacht *Drum* sank in 1986. The project was repeated with another group, for similar reasons, following the sinking of the cross-channel ferry *The Herald of Free Enterprise* in 1987.

Chapter Six

ARTHUR HUGHES The Copy, the Parody
and the Pastiche: Observations on
Practical Approaches to Critical Studies

> Copying makes us see more. Copying can change our minds.
> Copying can break our hearts. To copy is a serious responsibility. A
> copy must not make an artist turn in his grave. Some copying is
> useless. Some pretentious . . . . Jeffery Camp [1].

It was in 1970 that Dick Field, in *Change in Art Education*, sketched out
an agenda for the future in which he suggested that:

> If we are to function as artists—in the widest sense—in the adult
> world, we need something more in preparation than the incoherent
> experiences which are the way art education presents itself to many
> children and young people. What we need is a truer and deeper
> experience of art together with something more approaching a global
> grasp of art in the life of mankind . . . an understanding of art in
> these terms could be the objective of everyone's art education [2].

For Field this was no generalised slogan of the kind with which we
are all too familiar, but a quite specific and realisable objective grounded
in a deep understanding of both art and education. It was predicated
upon his primary belief in the educational value of the practice of art—
an anarchic, vital and 'untidy' activity which can be 'revealing at
different levels'. However, to Field, this truer and deeper experience of
art also implied types of knowledge and understanding which cannot be
attained purely through the making of artefacts. It went beyond the
boundaries of personal production and the kind of uncritical assumption
that encourages the unwary to believe that:

> The practice of art—the stimulus of drawing, painting and making
> things—leads . . . to a lifelong appreciation of works of art from
> different times and places and gives access to their meaning [3].

Almost twenty years later, there is a greater acceptance by art educators that without mediation the 'stimulus of drawing, painting and
making things' remains an incomplete experience. It remains, in Field's
terms, 'seen from within', and as such a partial experience with no
proven relationship to the goal of long-term appreciation of the work of
others. In order to attain this goal, the pupil must be encouraged to form
a more complete view of art, which involves seeing it 'from without'. Art
teachers have come to accept more readily that to gain access to art's
many meanings demands a capacity to analyse and reflect upon experience, and that it is the teacher's role to assist pupils to 'become self-
conscious about art' in order to develop a 'conscious understanding of
it' [4].

The nature of the mediation between the pupil's own creative experiences in art, and the wider world of ideas and their contexts, is an area of current practice where more research is urgently needed. In the absence of a range of appropriate procedures grounded in adequate theory, many teachers quite understandably concentrate on the attendant skills of studio activities. Personal art-making and not critical or analytical skills are generally seen as necessary and sufficient outcomes of good art teaching (although of course many would argue that successful art-making is dependent upon developed critical skills). Hence, because of this practical focus, the long-overdue return of *Critical Studies* into our schools has in fact heralded a return to the traditional practice of producing copies, pastiches and parodies of the works of others. *Critical Studies* has rapidly become subsumed within the dominant mode of art teaching, that is, taught in great measure through studio-based techniques.

It has recently been pointed out that 'the history of copying is part of the history of art' [5]. When carried out by one artist in relation to another's work, this is usually done in a spirit of affection and sometimes awe, as an attempt to fathom the 'secrets' of a work's facture, to make contact with the psychological mainspring of the other's creativity, or to 'share the experience trapped in the design' [6]. Few contemporary artists see the act of copying as an exercise in imitation, but most see it as a way of entering and occupying the presence of the admired work 'to see what the other chap has done' [7]. It is a critical, questioning activity which goes much deeper than the aping of superficialities of style or technique. Rather, it is a process of looking, in which, to use Francis Hoyland's words, the artist is 'likely to be confronted by the ferocious realisation of a masterwork', making contact with it 'at a very fundamental level' [8].

Transposed into the educational arena, this practice raises some crucial questions for the art teacher. Rarely, in a school context, will children copy originals, and usually the images in question will have been chosen by the teacher and may not previously have been seen by pupils. Therefore, prior to the act of copying, the pupil is faced by the quite daunting test of the imagination of having to recreate mentally from fragments of information (postcards, slides, details in books, teacher-description) a work of art which he or she has not actually seen in reality. Both medium and scale are likely to be at variance with the original, and even if the child employs the same media as those used by the mature artist, such technical insights that may accrue will have to be treated with scepticism unless the child understands something of the artist's processes and purposes. In many cases these cannot be deduced even in originals.

Furthermore, it must be remembered that, by any reasonably embracing definition, the processes employed by the artist—either consciously or unconsciously—will go far beyond mere manipulation of physical media, for

> Art is the product of an etiquette, and to neglect its framework of intellectual manners and reduce it to its physical data is an act of barbarism [9].

72

Sadly, acts of barbarism are all too commonplace in the *Critical Studies* classroom where copying and making pictorial equivalents can, if we are not careful, take the place of critical, analytical talk and the sharing of responses. It is essential that we go beyond this potentially limiting procedure and find ways to 'unpack' the creative processes of particular artists, possibly through reference to studio journals, diaries, the comments of contemporaries, and the results of historical research [10]. This is especially important if the child as 'copyist' is to be privy to some of the contextual knowledge which will enable him or her to know something of what Michael Baxendall has called the 'patterns of intention' underlying a particular work [11].

The main value for a pupil of copying from either an original or a reproduction is probably to be found in the fact that this process retains the child in the presence of the work for a sustained period of time. He or she is thus invited to contemplate its full complexity, and through this reflection, and the speculation it encourages, is also helped to assimilate knowledge of the work into his or her existing world picture. To paraphrase John Berger: a copy is not simply a representation of the copied work, but a visual record of the work of art *being looked at*. Whereas the sight of a work of art will register almost instantaneously, the graphic examination of that sight (copying) could take hours and

> involves, derives from, and refers back to, much previous
> experience of looking [12].

Nevertheless, as teachers we must remember that when pictures are used in the classroom, for whatever purpose, the context can have a profound influence upon the ways in which children perceive them. As Patrick Creber has pointed out:

> When a picture enters a classroom various things—comic,
> mechanical, or absurd—may happen to it. It is partly true to say
> that it is contaminated by its new setting but this hardly goes far
> enough. It is not merely spoilt or diminished; it is changed—it
> becomes *other*. When the keen, young or old, teacher bursts into his
> classroom on a Monday morning, the same fate may attend almost
> anything . . . that he carries under his arm [13].

Therefore when, as part of *Critical Studies*, the child is presented with a reproduction of Monet's *Water Lilies* to copy or in some other way parallel, it may not be received with the unalloyed enthusiasm the teacher, hotfoot from a weekend at Giverney, may expect, partly because

> The picture the teacher brings is not a gift. Nor does he just
> 'happen to have it with him'. He is there to teach and expects of
> them, in ways they too have learned to expect. Thus the picture is
> transmogrified into a text . . . . [14].

Experienced teachers adopt many strategies to maintain the freshness of children's responses to stimulus material. However, the act of recording or copying, over a prolonged period, may only serve to reinforce for the child the status of the picture as text. This may be especially so if the task of copying implies or leads to work that is, in Creber's words, 'text bound' or 'text dependent'—that is, lacking in any exploration of analogous experience. It would seem that this procedure is unlikely to yield rich fruits in terms of critical understanding, unless it is allied to other more-tentative and associative modes of response, such as many writers emphasise in relation to the development of critical awareness.

Appreciation involves the beholder in an active, searching process of progressive engagement with the work of art at its focus. In the classroom, without this *active* participation of the pupil, knowledge of works of art will remain 'out there'—as what Douglas Barnes has called *school knowledge* [15]. This is knowledge, provided by the teacher, which in its given form does not match the child's own world picture. To have meaning for children, 'school knowledge' must be turned into *action knowledge*, and thus become assimilated to the child's own purposes. This is a process that requires reflection, hypothesis and speculation, free from the pressures of conformity and correctness. Furthermore, the teacher's choice of works is crucial, for as Creber puts it:

> If pictures are to be of any value to me . . . they have to stir the
> mind, and the mind has to be free to be so stirred, which will not
> happen if notions of acceptable response interpose between the
> picture and the viewer . . . [16].

In short, it seems that for the attainment of truly meaningful knowledge we must not rush the child towards the 'single' acceptable explanation of a work of art, but must allow ample time for him or her to engage freer associations of ideas emanating from the consideration of the work. This is the chance to refer back to 'much previous experience of looking'. As Barnes reminds us, 'we observe not with our eyes alone but with our hypotheses' [17].

This process points up the real problem which will be experienced by many pupils faced with the task of copying a reproduction of a work of art, for this entails bringing 'life experience' to bear upon a work that already embodies the 'life experience' of the artist. The situation is further complicated by the fact that the teacher may not have any real access to the nature of this interaction, for when *any of us* regard visual images it is impossible to repress the brain's capacity to seek out meaning through analogy. The child's act of drawing or painting will thus take him or her on a path of personal re-creation based upon memories and recollections. The copy may mask, in its superficial resemblance to the original, the fact that through 'qualitative problem solving' the child may have voyaged into a rich inner world of personal associations and images. Continued emphasis by the teacher on the need to produce a 'finished' or 'acceptable' copy (in the teacher's own terms) may deny the child the very necessary space in which to explore, both in words and images, those rich personal meanings that are the raw material of knowing in the arts.

No-one has described this process better than Philip Rawson:

> To create, to respond to and understand drawing, we depend upon
> one great and fundamental faculty of the human mind, seldom
> discussed as it deserves: analogy . . . . It seems that as we live our
> lives a continuous activity of scanning and matching what we have

seen goes on in our minds. When we encounter one phenomenon our mind scans and matches it rhythmically with others we remember and know. It then connects that phenomenon with yet others—also with graphic forms already stocked in our memory from looking at pictorial images. The sharing of a common form constitutes analogy. By it we 'recognise' the phenomenon . . . . So each experience can be accompanied by a kind of memory resonance in our minds, which consists of a collection of near and more remote matches [18].

In his essay entitled 'The Eyes of Monet' John Berger gives us a graphic description of this process taking place in front of a painting by Monet of a lilac tree:

> Given the precision and the vagueness, you are forced to re-see the lilacs of your own experience. The precision triggers your visual memory, while the vagueness welcomes and accommodates your memory when it comes. More than that, the uncovered memory of your sense of sight is so acutely evoked, that other appropriate memories of other senses—scent, warmth, dampness, the texture of a dress, the length of an afternoon—are also extracted from the past. You fall through a kind of whirlpool of sense memories towards an ever receding moment of pleasure, which is a moment of total re-cognition [19].

The significance of this analogising capacity both to the maker and the beholder of art objects is also of great significance to teachers. If we encourage the kind of copying that aims for a near-likeness or a facsimile, we may be asking the pupil to engage in an activity which, although meant to foster knowledge about the works of others, is necessarily doomed to deny all but the most superficial understanding. Certain 'facts' about colour, composition, or the artist's 'handwriting' may certainly become more accessible; but I suggest that any understanding of deeper associative meanings, or of the cognitive processes that led to the work's outward appearance, will not easily be gained in this way. This knowledge must be gained, in large part, by tentative, exploratory and hypothetical activities, and involve the skilled exercise of classroom discussion and debate. If we settle for less, we risk inviting the child to learn about the making and significance of art objects through a form of artistic activity (copying) that ignores the rich analogical matching so essential to such an enterprise.

Acceptance of the educational limitations inherent in copying does not itself mean that there is no place for this activity in the classroom—it has, after all, been described as 'an intense way of looking'. As part of the teaching of practical art, copying can help extend the range of the pupils' awareness of elements such as colour, surface, and the nature of graphic marks. Robert Clement makes the point that:

> Even in reproduction it is difficult to observe any painting by Cézanne, van Gogh or Matisse without being aware of the way in which the artist uses both pigment and colour [20].

The same thing will not pertain to the reproduced works of many other artists; and I therefore suggest that two alternatives to the copy—the pastiche and the parody—may prove more fruitful in terms of the ultimate objective of encouraging critical understanding, as opposed to studio skills alone.

To be acceptable in terms of *Critical Studies* the notion of 'playing' with images, which is inherent in the making of pastiches and parodies, should not be allowed to demean the original work of art. On the contrary, it should be viewed as a serious form of visual enquiry from which the pupil will be led to greater understanding and knowledge of the original. Furthermore, it should not at any stage be seen as an alternative to the very demanding process of formalising thoughts, responses and critical judgements in language. Without using language, the teacher can have no certainty that the particular forms of meaning, made accessible through the visual arts, are being understood by children in ways that will inform their powers of discrimination. As teachers of *Critical Studies* our task is to help pupils form concepts from their experiences of the *particular* which they can subsequently develop into *general* principles applicable to a wide range of artistic contexts.

Examples abound of ways in which inventive teachers have introduced children to works of art by encouraging them to make their own versions. For example, in one infant school in the Midlands, each child was introduced to works by famous artists (selected by staff who were new to notions of 'art criticism'). The aim was to involve very young children *and their parents* in the activity of looking at pictures and enjoying work in local art galleries. Each infant produced equivalents 'in the styles of' well-known artists. Some images, such as those of Turner, van Gogh or Monet, were chosen principally for their painterly qualities. Others by Vasarely and Riley exemplified colour, pattern and

26 A 5 to 6-year-old's interpretation of 1 M W TURMER'S *Storm at Sea*; part of a study on the theme 'Great Artists'. Alumwell Infants' School, Walsall. (photo: Hughes, A)

27 A 5 to 6-year-old's interpretation of a landscape by VINCENT VAN GOGH; part of a study on the theme 'Great Artists', with special reference to depictions of weather. Alumwell Infants' School, Walsall.
(photo: Hughes, A)

sequence. Yet another group included works by Lowry and Bacon, and were used to help 6 and 7-year-olds investigate how emotions can be explored through images. By means of spoken and written language, and the introduction of a variety of paints, papers, brushes and markers, each class assembled a quite remarkable 'exhibition gallery'. Parents and friends were invited to a private view hosted by the children, who were most forthcoming in their explanations of their own works, and of the life histories of their chosen artists [21].

A recent project with fourth year junior children [22] included the presentation of reproductions of works by Degas, Renoir and Lautrec, as part of a study of 'the figure'. Each child was given one minute to describe to a partner a particular image of a figure. This meant that each one had to 'paint' a picture verbally for a colleague who was temporarily 'blind', paying particular attention to posture, dress and colours as depicted. From this exercise each was encouraged to talk freely about his or her own particular image, offering opinions about what had been discovered—a move towards action knowledge. Finally, each child made a personal rendering of the painting as described but not yet seen. The resulting lively, sensitive and very beautiful drawings

77

28 A 7-year-old's interpretation of a portrait by HENRI MATISSE; part of a study on the theme 'Great Artists'. Alumwell Infants' School, Walsall. (photo: Hughes, A)

revealed quite remarkable 'matches' with original masterworks, indicating perhaps the power of verbal discourse in the process of knowing in art.

Similar examples can be found in many secondary schools, although here the bias is often towards using these techniques to further pupils' practical skills rather than their powers of critical and analytical discrimination. One thinks of ideas books and study sheets for course projects on such typical themes as 'Water', 'Growth', or 'Disintegration', which very often contain copies and pastiches of the works of mature artists as visual resources for the young person's own imagery. This form

29 A first year Remedial group's collaborative interpretation of VINCENT VAN GOGH'S *Sunflowers*. John Beddoes Secondary School, Presteigne, Powys. (photo: Hughes, A)

of eclecticism is of course natural in adolescence when each individual is searching for his or her own identity. Many pupils in the later stages of a secondary school art course will incorporate into their own productions much that they admire in the work of others. It seems to me that this is normal, and we should only become uneasy when the young person either uses clichés and stereotypes as an avoidance of genuine enquiry, or looks no further than the most obvious starting points in art. It is this that may make us justifiably question the by now almost inevitable use of David Hockney's inventions whenever work is set on the theme 'Water'.

30   A third year mixed ability group's collaborative interpretation of a PAUL CÉZANNE *Still Life*. John Beddoes Secondary School, Presteigne, Powys.
(photo: Hughes, A)

The innovative and influential work of art educators such as Robert Clement [23] and Rod Taylor [24], has encouraged art educators throughout the country to introduce children of all ages to 'the real thing'; and there does seem to be mounting evidence that carefully-monitored and sensitively-taught practical work, derived from originals or illustrations, can play an important complementary role in *Critical Studies*. However, what must not be forgotten is that if *Critical Studies* is to develop and prosper in the curriculum it will ultimately rely as much upon modes of verbal expression and discourse as upon practical art-making. The former is essential if, in Dick Field's words, pupils are to gain understanding of art 'from without', and develop powers of discrimination, connoisseurship, and critical acuity.

Notes and References

1   CAMP, J. 1987.: in *Past and Present*. London, South Bank Centre; exhibition catalogue.
2   FIELD, D. 1970. *Change in Art Education*. London, Routledge & Kegan Paul.

3   DEPARTMENT OF EDUCATION AND SCIENCE. 1978. *Art in Junior Education.*
    London, Her Majesty's Stationery Office.
4   FIELD, *ibid.* Note 2.
5   HOYLAND, F. 1987. 'The Challenge of the Past'; in CAMP, *ibid.* Note 1.
6   MANN, S: *ibid.* Note 1, p. 50.
7   LEE, R: *ibid.* Note 1, p. 42.
8   HOYLAND, F: *ibid.* Note 1, p. 66.
9   BERGER, J. 1985. *The White Bird.* London, Chatto & Windus.
10 HUGHES, A: in TAYLOR, R. 1986. *Educating for Art.* London, Longman
    pp 262–3. Hughes discusses the gallery presentation of Ford Madox
    Brown's *The Last of England.*
11 BAXENDALL, M. 1985. *Patterns of Intention.* Cambridge, New Hampshire,
    Yale U.P.
12 BERGER, *ibid.* Note 9.
13 CREBER, J. W. P. *Voiceless Poems.* Exeter, Exeter University.
14 *Ibid.*
15 BARNES, D. 1976. *From Communication to Curriculum.* Harmondsworth,
    Penguin.
16 CREBER. *ibid.* Note 13.
17 BARNES. *ibid.* Note 15.
18 RAWSON, P. 1979. *Seeing through Drawing.* London, BBC Publications.
19 BERGER. *ibid.* Note 9.
20 CLEMENT, R. 1986. *The Art Teacher's Handbook.* London, Hutchinson.
21 Information from the Headteacher, Alumwell Infants' School, Walsall.
22 Information from Paula Holbrook and Colin Wilkes, c/o PGCE (Art and
    Design) Course, City of Birmingham Polytechnic.
23 CLEMENT. *ibid.* Note 20.
24 TAYLOR. *ibid.* Note 10.

Chapter Seven

JOHN BOWDEN Talking about Artworks: the Verbal Dilemma

Many art teachers display drawings, paintings, prints and other works—both originals and reproductions—around their schools, and most attempt to engage pupils in discussion about them. Some go further and encourage pupils to relate their own works to those on display, and it is clear that here verbal activities are regarded as primary methods of developing pupils' critical abilities. Talking about art is now an essential part of the typical art programme, given that *Critical Studies* is a compulsory GCSE requirement.

However, in my work with teachers it is apparent that there are valid reservations about this, or any other, procedure which involves pupils discussing or writing about works of art. Essentially this is a verbal process. The cognitive element is a significant factor in such procedures, and thus the more able pupils can dominate in debate, or easily absorb the critical model on offer. The less able may remain uncomprehending, and even those absorbing the model may find verbalising their judgements difficult.

Practical art activity, art teachers often argue, is a more democratic process. It is less clearly related to intellectual ability than are verbal critical activities; and thus associating pupils' *practical* work with that of mature artists should be an essential aspect of developing their critical abilities. But discussion cannot be divorced from this. Discussion of works of art, whether they come to schools as touring exhibitions, or are encountered on visits to galleries, is inevitable, and it is a significant new element for inclusion in schools' art programmes. For example, in the Department of Education and Science *Art in Secondary Education 11–16* survey of 1983 one school, in describing its 'analytical and critical approach' had as one major aim the desire that pupils

> could read a masterwork with that insight and understanding that
> would be necessary to read a novel.

It would be unfortunate, however, if this were to imply that a critical model might be taught in a manner similar to an English literature course. Pupils would be expected to manipulate it in a process of critical analysis. As I have argued elsewhere [1] this is potentially a dry and academic approach, and one which might well be mastered by the able pupil whilst the average child would encounter difficulties.

At a recent conference gallery education officers and teachers discussed the new GCSE skills and requirements, and in particular ways in which galleries might accommodate pupils on visits. The conference acknowledged the problems of engaging pupils in relevant discussion and of helping those charged with such responsibilities. It also noted the need to extend, develop and raise the quality of verbal debate, reinforcing what seems to be a general concern among teachers about the effective-ness, even the feasibility, of developing verbal exchange about works of art with the average pupil. Such teachers and gallery education officers, of course, have considerable stores of knowledge, both as practising artists and as art historians, so the problem is not one of teaching input. What was being identified was the gulf between those with an extensive art background and training, and the 'general public', whose knowledge of art criticism may be limited to the popular press denouncements of spending public money on piles of bricks.

It was in order to examine such difficulties—as encountered by groups without specialised art training—that I spent some time recording responses to selected sets of artworks from the *Original Works of Art Service* [2]. Groups of twenty or more pupils of various ages, comparative groups of primary and secondary teachers, senior citizens on recreational painting courses, and even members of the Townswomen's Guild, were observed over a five-year period. When invited to express a general opinion, or choose those artworks that were liked or disliked, their 'debate' was often discursive and brief. Subjects tended to make initial arbitrary judgements about their preferences, but extended or logical debate was unusual. It was obvious that most subjects had no 'critical model' to bring to bear, though a more coherent debate was apparent if it centred around a novel or a poem, perhaps because of past school training in English.

Some general aspects of behaviour were apparent early in my obser-vations. Many subjects felt there was a 'right' answer based on specialist knowledge or information, and wanted to know what the teacher or person chairing the discussion—who was thus regarded as an 'expert'—regarded as 'good' and 'bad'. One school in the DES survey, already mentioned, had claimed:

> Teachers were encouraged to declare their own positions, and be
> forthright about stating their own positions in debate, and most of
> all to urge pupils to acquire individual points of view.

However it was clear to me that this is only an effective strategy when working with students on, say, a PGCE course: with subjects lacking specialist art knowledge, the teacher's perspective tends to inhibit expression of the group's individual points of view. Opinions about artworks are of course just opinions: some are informed and some are not. The process of criticism does not prove absolutely the merit of one work relative to another, nor does it rely on scientific logic. Two groups of equally well-informed critics, after lengthy debate, will probably reach different conclusions. Indeed groups may radically change their own views as time passes. It was a first and important lesson for the groups I worked with that their judgements were as valid as those of the 'expert'. Whilst it is to a certain extent true that complicated analyses of works of art are often made by critics and reviewers, the teacher needs to emphasise—in order to encourage debate—that the uninitiated can express valid views without 'expert' knowledge. The view that art criticism is solely the province of people of learning has done much to inhibit the average person's enjoyment of art.

In my study it was clear that comparing 'like with like' was much easier than, for example, comparing a painting with a sculpture, a ceramic object or a woven craftwork. The latter comparison is clearly difficult for the uninitiated and in my work it proved unwise. On the other hand, severe limitation of the range of work on offer, such as comparison of a set of drawings by a single artist, so limited the range of debate as to be unproductive. The central problem seemed to be a tendency for the debate to swing aimlessly between conflicting arguments, from discussion about the colour scheme of a painting, for instance, to arguments about its meaning, and then to become even more confused by interjections about the way the artist had applied the paint. Louis Arnaud-Reid noted this phenomenon when he wrote:

> We have to establish by careful analysis that the disagreements are real disagreements—and with a complex object like a work of art it is easy for two people who hastily think they disagree to find they are talking about and emphasising quite different things so that their talking has been at cross purposes [3].

Elliot Eisner and Vincent Lanier, among others, have divided the process of aesthetic analysis into separate domains. However theirs are complex models intended for the scrutiny and understanding of the art professional. What seemed to me to be needed was a simple structure, based on categorising central aspects of the debate about artworks, derived from the language and observations of the uninitiated, which could act as the basis for a teaching strategy in guiding the debate through the cross-purposes that Louis Arnaud-Reid describes. Such a model should thus be more easily comprehensible to the average person, and be simple enough to be offered to pupils in practical discussion of artworks. To this end I recorded at length the reactions of my subject groups, and noted that they fell into six simple, discrete categories. Whereas Eisner and Lanier have presented more complex models, my intention was to devise a structure that could be absorbed by the typical participant, rather than the pupil of above average ability with a great interest in art. My six categories are 'criteria of judgements', identified as the (a) *arbitrary*; (b) *skill/technique*; (c) *materials*; (d) *expressive*; (e) *visual language*; and (f) *contextual* criteria.

The first, and often the only one used by some subjects, is a 'non-aesthetic' or *Arbitrary* criterion of judgement. Representative responses here would be 'I like it (a brightly-coloured abstract painting) because it would go in my bedroom', or 'I like it (a picture of a cat) because I like cats'. In both of these examples the aesthetic qualities are incidental; the judgement in the first case precludes challenge by others, unless they know the room in question; and in the second case discussion is likely to develop into a debate about cats rather than the aesthetic content of the artwork. Though such statements are valid as bases for preference, they are closed and unhelpful as catalysts for discussion. My first aim in my study was to move subjects on from this position to a consideration of other categories. Elliot Eisner has written:

> Preference for style in art requires no education or sophistication.
>
> As in taste, in matters of preference there can be no dispute.

Anyone can have, and is entitled to his own preference or taste.

Judgement is another matter [4].

In my second category a work of art would be admired for its representational qualities, the artist praised for his skill and technique in depicting a real situation in a life-like manner, through skills in controlling the tools or the medium. Evidence of draughtsmanship and observation of details would be praised. The emphasis in discussion would be on the manner in which a painting 'could be mistaken for a photograph', in admiration for the way in which certain artists have the capacity to act as colour cameras. It was clear in my observations that some subjects' perceptions of the function of a work of art were so dominated by this criterion as to lead them to eliminate from consideration any works— particularly abstract works—that did not immediately offer evidence of it.

The *materials* criterion concerns the ways in which the material sets limits, or is used in an experimental or specific manner, to the extent of becoming an important aspect of the artist's work or the subject's response to it. In my study, for instance, the thickness or translucency of paint was sometimes a source of delight for its own sake. At the same time much criticism of a perjorative nature was reserved for artists who 'threw paint onto the canvas': this was often voiced by those subjects whose praise for work often concentrated on the *skill/technique* criterion.

The *expressive* criterion is concerned with the subject's 'feeling response' to the artwork. This would include the capacity of a work of art to transmit feelings inherent in its subject-matter—for example a depiction of a sad old lady—or the capacity of certain colours or forms to evoke specific moods or emotions in the viewer. Imaginative works charged with mood or atmosphere fall into this category. Tolstoy wrote:

> Art is a human activity consisting in this; that one man consciously, by means of external signs, hands on to others feelings he has lived through, so that others are infected by these feelings, and experience them [5].

The formal qualities of the work of art, or the *visual language* in use, were often the subject of debate. This could be as simple as an observation about a 'pleasing colour scheme', though a balanced composition or contrasting shapes might have been commented on also. This aspect has been observed by Jack Hobbs when he noted that an artist was

> more concerned with arranging the visual elements of a painting— colours, shapes, lines, textures and spaces—than he was with the recreation of a particular scene [6].

The *contextual* criterion does, however, without doubt require a background knowledge of the schools and styles of art. Such information as the nature of the work produced in a particular era, why it was produced, and by whom, can be the subject of scholarship without enhancing our understanding of its aesthetic value. This *Contextual* criterion of judgement is hardly ever offered by the uninitiated, for obvious reasons.

While I accept that my basic model might be regarded as simplistic by those with an art training, I emphasise its relevance for pupils and adults without significant abilities and knowledge. It proves reasonably easy to familiarise such individuals with its elements, enabling various strategies to be introduced for extending debate and reducing Arnaud-Reid's 'cross-purpose' talking. Most works of art invite criticism from all aspects of this simple critical model: however, some tend to exhibit one of its aspects strongly. For instance, much discussion of a Surrealist work by Magritte will concern its *expressive* or imaginative qualities; while an abstract work by Sam Francis might more usually be discussed from its *material* perspective.

I found it possible to select a range of works in which each seemed to concentrate discussion in a particular category. For instance I would include a work in which the artist had concentrated on representation of the external world (criterion b), one which depicted the emotional state of the subject (d), another primarily concerned with the abstract organisation of colour and form (e), and one showing evidence of a major artistic concern for the use of materials (e). I would then proceed by asking questions designed to emphasise aspects of each discrete category: Which was the most realistic? Which most clearly expressed the feelings of the artist? Which concentrated on pattern? In which had the artist most enjoyed the properties of the material? Such questions tended to create the basis for a debate that would concentrate on each of the categories in turn and in some coherent order. Though not all subjects would agree on particular interpretations, the very act of disagreeing would ensure that debate became focused on a specific category.

An alternative method would be to permit free, unfocused discussion of a range of artworks, and use the subjects' statements to prompt introduction of the categories. For instance, if someone were to talk about a colour scheme being 'pleasant', this would introduce the *visual language* category, and invite discussion of the artwork's other formal structure. If the thickness of paint were mentioned, this would offer a lead-in to discussion of the *materials* category. Teaching responsiveness and neutrality are crucial to the success of this approach, in leading the group from an *arbitrary* standpoint into simple but structured critical processes.

It has already been suggested that most works of art operate simultaneously in more than one area: this is complicated, in addition, by the fact that it is not always possible to divine the intentions of the artist. These issues may form the basis for a spirited but more-focused debate, leading participants to make distinctions between works they 'like' and those they regard as 'artistically good', permitting themselves the luxury of an 'arbitrary' standpoint while reserving rights to aesthetic criticism. It was clear from my work with groups over a period that the level of debate became more coherent and sustained. A critical study of the works took place in an unforced way, using terminology that was comprehensible to subjects, and that they could bring to bear on other works at other times. Adults as well as school-children began to understand the distinction between a balanced aesthetic judgement and an arbitrary statement of taste.

Most important in my view was the fact that the process was a non-didactic one, in which the average subject was able to express his or her opinions through free verbal exchanges. While it is still open to criticism for potentially permitting the domination of superior verbal skills, it avoids the transmission of a complex critical model through a formal, chronological art history inappropriate to the typical pupil or recreational student. I do not propose that talking about works of art should supplant the making of art in our schools, but I do feel that verbal exchanges are likely to become more and more important in future education, and that the strategy I have outlined may control and develop the quality of initial debate.

Notes and References

1 See BOWDEN, J. 1984. *Using Pictures with Children*. Association of Art Advisers.
2 This Service, now renamed the *Educational Resource Service*, has a collection of some 800 artworks collected over the past thirty years, which are circulated around four contributing Yorkshire Authorities. The works are almost entirely contemporary though mostly of traditional style, and are largely by unknown artists.
3 ARNAUD-REID, L. 1969. *Meaning in the Arts*. London, Allen & Unwin.
4 EISNER, E. 1972. *Educating Artistic Vision*. New York, Macmillan; p. 138.
5 TOLSTOY, L. (1930) *What is Art?*. Oxford, Oxford University Press; p. 108.
6 HOBBS, J. 1985. *Art in Context*. 3rd ed. Harcourt Brace Jovanovitch; p. 15.

Chapter Eight

KATY MACLEOD Gallery and School: Art Study Programmes

Beyond the gallery tour

Gallery education is mushrooming at a tremendous pace. Hundreds of thousands of gallery visits are made annually by untold numbers of school children [1]. For the vast majority of them, the gallery tour will represent their only experience of learning in a gallery, as the tour represents the backbone of education provision in galleries in Great Britain. Alternative education provision, which undoubtedly exists, is spasmodic, under evaluated and under researched.

In the USA, gallery tours have long been questioned as the dominant strategy for encouraging children to take an interest in what galleries have to offer:

> . . . Dissatisfaction with the traditional group tour, in which docents herd children through the museum, lecturing all the way, is not new, but increasing numbers of art museum educators have begun to despair of it. To many museum educators . . . the traditional tour often seems to impose a passive learning situation on children, to give them irrelevant information, and, even in the hands of the most sympathetic and stimulating lecturer or docent, to be antithetical to the idea that children learn best through participation, discovery, and the stimulation of their natural curiosity . . . [2].

'Participation', 'discovery' and 'stimulation' are limited when teacher/lecturer guides the flow of information, directs any exchange between viewer and object viewed and generally intercedes between the learner and his source [3]. A shift in responsibility needs to be effected from teacher to child. Such a shift is of course risk taking and runs counter to those education strategies we've all adopted, of 'active encouragement' of the wrong sort when the going gets rough [4].

This is how John Holt talks of our familiar failures:

> . . . almost all children fail . . . they fail to develop more than a tiny part of the tremendous capacity for learning, understanding, and creating with which they were born and of which they made full use during the first two or three years of their lives.
>
> Why do they fail?
>
> They fail because they are afraid, bored, and confused. They are afraid, above all else, of failing, of disappointing or displeasing the many anxious adults around them, whose limitless hopes and expectations for them hang over their heads like a cloud.
>
> They are bored because the things they are given and told to do in school are so trivial, so dull, and make such limited and narrow

demands on the wide spectrum of their intelligence, capabilities and talents [5].

The gallery tour so readily falls into both these pits—anxious school teacher, anxious gallery teacher, each intent on not 'drawing a blank' and so keeping the pitch far below the children's capabilities. After all, the gallery environment itself may impose a level of anxiety unless this is alleviated through an activity where the child him/herself sets up a measure of control over his/her surroundings, staking a claim to his/her place there [6].

However, this *is* the preferred form of education in galleries, a common currency acceptable throughout education. In fact children often view with suspicion the teacher who attempts to negotiate a shift in the balance of responsibility: 'Call yourself a teacher, Miss?' comes from my own repertoire of engaging sayings from those I've 'taught'.

It is, of course, easier to come to terms with the need for information to be transferred at all costs, far harder to cling to the educative ideal of insisting that learning is effected through an exchange where the method, content and outcome are *not* predetermined by teacher.

> Yet the group tour remains the backbone of most museum education programs, partly because changing the status quo requires more energy than preserving it, but more important, because there is no guarantee that current substitutions for the traditional one-time lecture tour will be more effective [7].

Collaboration

Galleries and schools need to collaborate, not simply about the detailing of gallery visits, but about the whole question of effective education through art. (What is it? How does it happen?)

> Taking into account the outstanding variety in the way school visits are organised, some being part of carefully constructed programmes of related study, some being purely off the cuff and casual, educational visits are generally of the slot-in kind! Schools come with their courses sewn up, visit the gallery, take what the gallery has on offer, and go. The gallery may be unaware of the overall purpose of the visit and may not be fully informed about follow-up sessions [8].

Of course the loss of opportunity resulting from the slot-in visit works both ways: the school makes too narrow a claim on the gallery's resources, and the gallery pitches its tour—or whatever it's offering—largely in the dark.

Collaboration should represent a clear attempt to ensure that both gallery and school understand and appreciate each other's context, not just on a superficial level, but down to the numerous unspoken differences which often obstruct working together.

> Galleries like Arnolfini deal in changing contexts. Arnolfini presents 'the best of the new', 'the innovatory'. 'New' contexts are made for young artists whose work is grouped in exhibitions like 'Objects and Sculpture' or 'Style in the Seventies'. The 'Style in the Seventies'

exhibition mushroomed a style which, once the exhibition tour ended and the context for that style was withdrawn, disappeared. Schools, on the other hand, are required to develop strategies which enforce stability. One of the crucial concerns for any head at the moment is how to ensure a developing and deepening relationship between the schools' curricula and the requirements of external examinations. (It is, after all, difficult to conceive of any kid being set in the way of a bright future without a single CSE, O- or A-level.) However, in the examination system changes are slow; two years for changes to work through the system and reviews are not annual affairs.

In Arnolfini then, there's a rapid shifting of gears, in schools a more even and stabilised pace [9].

Each context creates its own expectations. This coupled with differences in training and education, adds to the potential barriers to fruitful co-operation.

Whenever museum and school people anywhere try to work together a difficult problem surfaces. Museum educators nowadays generally pride themselves on their flexibility, inventiveness, and conception of the student as a potentially creative being. Most school people find this attitude a sloppy promise for the business of teaching, priding themselves on their ability to undertake and complete a project in which students realise some of their potential. Most museum educators in turn find this emphasis on achievement rigid and narrow [10].

Within this collaborative framework, the gallery provides a different kind of teacher, 'the real thing' (i.e. the work itself), exhibiting or non-exhibiting artists, a different time continuum from that offered by the school timetable, different resources generally. The school provides 'fully professional' teachers, children who know nothing of art world assumptions, a 'live' resource for the gallery to record, note and learn from, particularly through their expectations derived from the 'normal' world of parents, families and school rather than the all absorbing world of the arts.

Collaboration must take place on the base rung of the 'purposes, premises and patterns' of the programme [11]. However, this is difficult to set up unless collaboration has also taken place across the superstructure of the Local Education Authority, the Regional Arts Association and through the Head/Director of the institutions wishing to collaborate. To this end a preliminary strategy must be carefully conceived and go through those channels which affect arts and education policy decisions.

Collaboration does not represent a gloss to smooth over potential differences of approach between gallery and school. It is fundamental to an attempt to bring about change, to prove that the gallery can be more than simply as one survey found, an ad hoc teaching aid, having no effect on the school's curriculum and certainly of no use during examination years [12].

Collaboration has been called for, for a very long time [13] but there is still little evidence that it does take place. It is however, absolutely essential if progress in this aspect of arts education is to be made. Even in the number game, it makes sense:

> Educate one teacher and you improve the opportunity for 30 plus
> pupils to make concrete connections between icons and ideas,
> between your museum and their lives [14].

Substitute gallery teacher for 'teacher' and duplicate the numbers in suitable fashion, and the reasons for collaborative practice become evident.

The role of the professional artist

> The arts are not only to do with the development of practical skills.
> They are to do with exploring ideas and feelings, issues and events
> that concern artists both as individuals and as members of society
> . . . [15].

> Contact with the contemporary arts, or with the living world of the
> art of the past would seem to be an indispensable source of personal
> stimulus and nourishment. A teacher's personal involvement in the
> processes of art is likely to give his teaching relevance and vitality—
> also teaching will become neither perfunctory nor mechanical in his
> hands. Like any other system—organic, electronic, or social—an
> arts department without effective and vital links with its
> environment will suffer progressive breakdown [16].

Art practice has to feed on a myriad of different sources. The inclusion of artists within art study programmes has two distinct purposes: one, to ensure that the professional practice of art is understood ('£500 for that. It's a bloody con, Miss') and a balanced perspective of art practice given, and two, to ensure that whatever art is encountered can be discussed with artists who have the ability to communicate 'the cementing, healing, bridging role' of art [17]. The inclusion of professional artists within art programmes also ensures a useful balance between art theory and art practice. Luke Finkelstein, for instance, also believes art museum educators get it wrong: they do not understand the 'true meaning' of art and are 'endemically deficient in a philosophic view of their own state of knowledge'. He may well be right. At any rate, the presence of art theory ensures: firstly, that standards presented to the participating children are not limited to their own or their peers' achievements; secondly, that art criticism naturally takes its place, along with aesthetics as integral to an understanding of 'visual' art. This seems logical to the point of obviousness but so many children are led to believe that art is about the *activity* of art only:

> I had hoped that it would not be necessary to tell the pupils that the
> thinking was more important than the product alone, and that if the
> thinking process was correct, then the object would take care of
> itself [18].

'The thinking process' here dictates the level and pitch of learning. Underpinning art study programmes should be an understanding of the need for learning to concern itself with problem solving.

One of the most active ways of coming to know about things is via the Method of Interaction. We come to know what a lemon is like by breaking it open and sucking it . . . We come to know about cooking by interacting with food and cooking utensils . . . The point about the Method of Interaction is that we induce events in the real world (not just on paper) which make the real thing real to us [19].

There is no point in inviting huge numbers of children to visit galleries to see 'the real thing' *unless* they can appropriate its meanings in their own terms. The material presence of the work itself *means* nothing if the child does not understand of what that presence is composed [20].

Case studies reviewed

'Gallery and School: Art Study Collaborative Programmes' was the title given to a research project based on five art study programmes run jointly by Arnolfini and five schools within Avon [21]. The research was of the 'responsive' or 'illuminative' type [22] and as such 'responded' to the contexts of gallery and school and the changing needs of the participants. No special gallery programme was sought or devised; no special school groups or timetabling or syllabus arrangements were required. The art study programmes were expressly designed to fit into existing school and gallery structures, to extend rather than radically reshape them.

The intention of each programme was 'locally' different, that is superficially, there were few similarities in terms of programme content. However, the overall intention was in each case to secure an enriched experience of art study and art practice through drawing on the strengths of both gallery and school through sustained, rather than limited collaboration [23]. In school A, an inner city junior school, the intention was 'to work with colour to extend the children's use of visual language'.

The objectives were:

1   By careful planning, to build up the children's confidence to make sense of the subject under consideration in their own terms.
2   To ensure that this confidence provided a business-like and casual encounter with 'high art' thus enabling the children to claim a space in the gallery and work without distractions caused by anxiety.
3   To ensure that each child was prepared to work with paintings which are full of meanings not just in terms of content, but in terms of *the way* the marks are put down; that is, the organised *sense* of the paintings.

The overall objective therefore was to develop the child's own visual vocabulary in order to help him/her to look and respond effectively to his/her own work, peers' work and to artists' work.

Within this framework, certain teaching strategies were adopted:

1   A rigorous and prescriptive attention to a professional understanding of materials, coupled with a decided lack of any prescriptive guidance about the child's own products (i.e. the palette had to be understood in a professional way but no guidance was ever given as to the shape a particular piece of work should take.)
2   Following from this, no responsibility was taken off the child's own shoulders in relation to his/her own work. All decisions about the way

each part of the programme was to be undertaken were taken by the children themselves.

3 Assessment too was taken to be the responsibility of the individual child or the group.

4 A consistent approach to teaching in school, in the school grounds and in the galleries.

5 Rigorous attention to the *process* of making to preclude any lack of comprehension about a particular mode of working, i.e. abstraction.

6 A combinative approach of rigorous attention to the detail of each phase of the programme with a complete openness of mind about *how* these were interpreted by the children. There was no question of the work being discussed in terms of being 'good' or 'bad'.

The findings from this case study illuminated many possibilities as we watched children develop through the programme:

> . . . museums—conceived as environments for free (i.e. non-coercive) learning—might be able to take on a dramatic new significance. Among other things, they might be able to offer learning experiences of a qualitatively different and richer kind from those which a conventional classroom offers. Whereas classroom learning tends to be *accretive* (with the progressive accumulation of a stockpile of other people's facts and opinions and discoveries, etc.), museum learning could be *renovative*—renovative of specific misunderstandings, and renovative, more generally, of the individual's whole personality. This possibility exists because environments that can potentiate free non-coercive learning are environments that can potentiate, in the participants, a process of self-healing and self-understanding [24].

Findings from school D illuminated starkly two problem areas for collaborative practice within the GCE art course: one, the obsession with marketable results and two, the acceptance of any school project as a task set by someone else, according to standard criteria—and to be assessed by the same. This passive acceptance of external criteria as the *only* way of channelling and assessing work is highly questionable. This school, like many others, has no internal school syllabus: the syllabus followed is that set for the A-level exam. Is it inevitable that students being taught according to these guidelines, will find difficulty in responding to primary source material which is not of 'the required type'?

The implications here are, of course, manifold. The intention of the programme had been 'to use colour to introduce the students to the processes of abstraction' and hence to facilitate a greater breadth of understanding of the visual arts which is essential for mature development. We found the students did not wish to step outside what *they* took to be the 'normal' A-level syllabus and were extremely hesitant about taking on the work involved in opening out horizons.

However, it was *only* at the point of hesitancy that students were able to develop. This was again underlined through the findings from school B. The intention here was 'to increase the students' understanding of drawing through an understanding of dance and movement.'

This is an excerpt from one student's notebook:

. . . there had to be a different way of capturing the movement. Movement is nothing without something to move, i.e. the body. But the body on its own is not movement. That is, a pose or even a series of poses are not movement. It is more the displacement of the air surrounding the body. So I thought of it being extremely dark and there being lights attached to the dancer's hands and feet and head and a very slow shutter speed camera. This gave me the streak of the path of the limbs.

Then I turned the lights on. I drew in the limbs to go with the movement. This rather gives the effect of one of those night post cards of London or Paris where you can't see the cars but you see where they've been by their head and tail lights.

It's not perfect (or even close) but I surprised even myself. Consequently I finished the evening feeling a lot more confident than I had begun with the problem both of the movement and that awful chalk and charcoal.

We found this kind of risk taking essential to any meaningful progress:

In Britain in particular, educators are depressingly anxious 'to protect' the young or limit them from access to challenging ideas [25].

We also found through school C in particular (but all schools generally) the enormous importance of the student him/herself setting up a measure of control within the learning context. Here the intention was 'to illuminate and enrich art studies by seeing art history through artists' eyes'. The programme hinged on artists being invited into the school to talk about for example, the impact of Cubism on their work, and visits being made to Arnolfini to talk to the exhibiting artists about their work and influences exerted on it.

Here the turning point for most students came when *they* had been encouraged to put their own sensibilities on the line: What did *they* think? How did *they* view this? What is this about? How do *they* relate it to this? And so on.

It was at this point that one student from school C changed her whole attitude to art and decided to attempt to get to art college. And it was *only* after this point that the students felt sufficiently confident to seek out questions they wanted answered. During the two gallery visits *they* dictated the flow of conversation and insisted on talking about art college and what it was like to be an artist. The work itself was only briefly discussed. At the time, this seemed a case of a wasted opportunity but on reflection, this does indicate the students' need to relate the programme to their own lives. In this sense, they all learnt more about themselves, in their attempts to measure up these artists' experiences to their own.

The most consistent finding and the general characteristic of all the art study programmes was the sustained and marked growth in confidence of most of the participants. (It is, of course, impossible to quantify this finding.) Here is the teacher's assessment of one child's progress from school A: 'Errol made an immediate response to the sessions, and out of all the children got the most enjoyment from the project [26]. It was very important for Errol to have experienced the success that the project brought him. Success is not something he associates very often with school.'

There is no doubt in my mind that this is the direct result of the participating artist's general approach to making and working with art. In answer to 'indicate the major advantages . . .' (one of a series of 'assessment' questions asked at the end of the programme) she replied, 'Anyone deeply involved in any subject is worth talking to and working with because of their enthusiasm for their subject. It's good for the children to see someone excited by something they love. Maybe it would stimulate a germ of a passion in the mind of a child. In the use of artists, no talking can convey as much inside knowledge as the act of having made art—the nitty gritty of materials and process—that's worth sharing with children.'

31   Having fun with work produced at an exhibition of Stephen Farthing's work at Arnolfini (school A). (photo: Macleod, K)

32   Concentration on the work in hand at an exhibition of Bill Henderson's work at Arnolfini (school A). (photo: Macleod, K)

33   Bill Henderson discussing his work with sixth formers of school C. (photo: Macleod, K)

Again the concentration is on *how* an artist works. This is absolutely central to a child's commitment to looking at artists' work. Children may be mute in front of a finished product. What can it mean if they are unprepared for the encounter? When this group of children went to see Bill Henderson's huge abstract paintings, not one of them wanted to know what they meant, because we had prepared them for their own encounter with Bill's work *to make sense* in their own terms [27].

In answer to 'Why is it important to take children to galleries?', the artist responded, 'To let them develop a confident approach to using galleries and just to make art a familiar part of their lives; to develop a critical eye—only possible with lots of looking at a wide range of art'.

Our intention, and the main intention throughout all the art study programmes was to make the activity of going to galleries seem as commonplace as going to the local swimming pool, and no less easy.

A general finding

It needs to be said that contact with the contemporary arts must be sustained and in-depth to counterbalance the challenging seduction of our 'mega visual culture', as Peter Fuller calls it [28]. Meaningful contact with professional artists requires a dramatic shift of values from rating the apparent and marketable to the multi-layered, and sometimes in-articulate. We are, after all, conditioned to consume and applaud the obvious, even though this may be cleverly camouflaged in images of multiple identities—the Benson and Hedges advertisements, for instance.

This does not mean that 'high art' is to be encountered as more mean-ingful than advertising, in a self conscious way, but that the visual arts should be recognised for what they are—ordinary and everyday, but profound and searching at the same time. Thus Bill Henderson recom-mended follow-up sessions for the students, 'I would have loved to have seen some of them putting two or three colours on the same brush, as I do, and having to take a deep breath, (how? will it work? what shall I do with it?) and an instantaneous decision to put those colours some-where and make them 'play' amongst the colours and marks put down before! If they could get into the spirit of *that*, it becomes a very exciting business.'

Art practice *is* both simple and profound. One only has to touch on, say, Francis Bacon's work to view the obvious truths of the absolutely rational and simple explanation of why he uses medical textbooks as sources for his work—that he's interested in the human body—to the 'inarticulate' explanation which is to do with his obsessive curiosity and anxiety about the human condition in both its physical and spiritual dimensions. (Where *is* the spiritual element located in the body?) This ordinariness and specialness of art is what needs to be communicated to people of school age. Art is for everyone. Everyone has a stake in being 'an artist' but this does not mean a sloppy liberalness diminishing art's special claims. Quite the reverse, art is fed and sustained through reaching a wider network of young people in this way.

The one triumph of the art study programmes was that even if the specialness of art did not always register, the ordinariness of it did:

> These educational visits arranged by teachers, and the special performances for school children put on by many theatres, concert halls and opera houses have, for all their virtues, one drawback. It is that they are perceived as 'special' by the pupils involved: the event can be treated, especially by working class pupils, as something so extraordinary that it has no implications or relevance for their ordinary lives, in which there are no such visits. These 'special performances' may be sealed up and cut off from ordinary life. But if these visits are to be truly effective, there must be some transfer so that visiting a theatre, gallery, opera house or concert hall is a natural habit, something that can be undertaken quite spontaneously on the pupils' own initiative. I believe we have paid too little attention to this in our educational policies for the arts [29].

Notes and References

1   The National Gallery, London, tours in excess of 50,000 schoolchildren annually.

2   NEWSOME, B. Y. and A. Z. SILVER (eds). 1978. *The Art Museum as Educator: a Collection of Studies as Guides to Practice and Policy.* University of California Press, p. 267.

3   There are so many alternative approaches here. See John Bowden's essay (Chapter 7).

4   This applies across the education spectrum. See CORNOCK, S. 1984. Learning Strategies in Fine Art, *Journal of Art and Design Education*, Vol. 3, No. 2; pp. 141–59.

5   HOLT, J. 1964. *How Children Fail.* Harmondsworth, Penguin, p. 9.

6   Misunderstandings in this area of education are absolutely rife. Robert Witkin cites the teacher who is bitterly disappointed when 'his' children fail to respond positively to a half hour visit to an exhibition he has enjoyed himself. See WITKIN, R. 1974. *The Intelligence of Feeling.* London, Heinemann, p. 108.

7   NEWSOME and SILVER; *ibid.* Note 2, p. 267.

8   MACLEOD, K. 1983. *Education Supplement.* Bristol, Arnolfini Gallery.

9   *Ibid.* Arnolfini is a multi-arts complex in Bristol, which houses two large galleries and a programme of exhibitions of exclusively contemporary work.

10 NEWSOME and SILVER; *ibid.* Note 2, p. 271.

11 See REGNE, B. 1978. From Object to Idea, *Museum News* Vol. 56, No. 3; pp. 45–47.

12 See LEFROY, J. A. 1967. Museums and Educational Institutions, *Museums Journal* Vol. 67, No. 2.

13 For an elderly and notable source see SCHOOLS COUNCIL. 1972. *Pterodactyls and Old Lace: Museums in Education.* London.

14 See REGNE; *ibid.* Note 11, pp. 45–47.

15 CALOUSTE GULBENKIAN FOUNDATION. 1983. *Report.*

16 ROSS, M. 1975. *Art and the Adolescent.* Schools Council Working Paper No. 54, p. 44.

17 See FINKELSTEIN, L. 1978. Art and the Museum; in NEWSOME and SILVER; *ibid.* Note 2, p. 589.

18 POPE, N. 1978. *Artists in Schools Project.* Whitechapel Art Gallery, London and Ryde School, Isle of Wight.

19 See LEWIS, B. 1980. The Museum as an Educational Facility, *Museums Journal* Vol. 80, No. 3, (pp. 151–57), p. 154.

20 Much more research needs to be done in this area, preferably based on non-purpose designed centres, for although the work of the Drumcroon Arts Centre (see Chapter 3) is excellent, the facilities are so specialised as to make findings there difficult to reapply.

21 This study was the result of the NSAE/Berol Bursary Award (1983), and arose out of the extension of gallery-based programmes at Arnolfini.

22 See PARLETT, M. and D. HAMILTON. 1972 Evaluation as Illumination: a New Approach to the Study of Innovative Programmes, *Occasional Paper No. 9*. University of Edinburgh, Centre for Research in Educational Services.

23 Each programme lasted a minimum of 10 weeks and was designed to be taken up as part of both the school's art(s) syllabus and the gallery education programme.

24 LEWIS. *ibid.* Note 19, p. 155.

25 STENHOUSE, L. 1975. *An Introduction to Curriculum Research and Development*. London, Heinemann, p. 29.

26 Errol, a West Indian, had been expelled from his last school for disruptive behaviour. He had a measured IQ of 67. Discussion with gallery colleagues has led me to understand that it is very often the under-achievers who benefit most readily from this kind of work.

27 Bill Henderson is the artist whose work was being exhibited at Arnolfini for a substantial part of the time allocated to the art study programmes. He played an active part in three of them.

28 See FULLER, P. 1980. *In Defence of Art: Beyond the Crisis of Art*. Writers and Readers.

29 HARGREAVES, D. H. 1983. Dr Brunel and Mr Downing: Reflections on Aesthetic Knowing, in: 'The Arts: a Way of Knowing', *Curriculum Issues in Arts Education* Vol. 4, p. 127.

Chapter Nine

BRANDON TAYLOR Art History in the Classroom: a Plea for Caution

The recent wholesale retreat from child-centred methods in art education is bringing about—or has been brought about by—a new interest in art as a teachable, learnable, examinable subject. Practitioners of the 'cognitive-developmental' approach are now engaged upon a considerable programme of research aimed at finding out what can be taught about art and the practice of art at different levels of the school curriculum, and, correspondingly, how much of the previous paradigm of art-as-expression can be jettisoned as worthless baggage. As readers will know, the results are varied, challenging, sometimes inconsistent, but always heavy with the implication that art and art practice are there to be learnt, possibly as a core subject in general education or possibly as a major fourth addition to the still-predominant three Rs.

This is neither the time nor the place to launch an assessment of the 'cognitive-developmental' approach and all its various findings and prescriptions. Art historians, however, are bound to be intrigued by recent investigations into two proximate but actually distinguishable questions. The first is simply what types of art images are to be used in the classroom?—and here I remind you of the fact that the choice is potentially vast; that selectivity is unavoidable. And the second question concerns how these images are to be used—for what purpose, and by what methods? It is excellent that some debate on these important questions should now be under way once more. But our discussion must inevitably have some reference to a newer type of understanding that is being developed within art history itself, an understanding which for some time now has insisted on the historical rootedness of works of art (and all other constructed images) not merely in the emotional system of the artist, but in the social, economic and ideological interchange of the society as a whole. This understanding is not fixed or immutable, thankfully. But art historians are not going to remain happy for long, I suspect, if visual images continue to be used indiscriminately in the classroom merely in the service of an unstructured notion of 'appreciation'; nor, what is worse but no less likely, given the present attack on teachers' resources by government, if artworks are paraded merely out of convenience, or for reasons stemming primarily from the taste of the teacher.

This may be a useful moment therefore to voice some fears about the dangers of unreflective art history in schools, as yet too little thought out, and in some cases provided at too early an age for the children concerned. I argue that we need to abandon the practice of studying received 'masterpieces' alone, such as can be obtained in reproduction from museum bookstalls; and that *modern* culture in particular, far from representing the 'art of our time', constitutes a specialist minority culture that is frequently inappropriate, both technically and emotionally, for presentation to the growing child. Images of a much wider and more accessible kind must form the basis of primary and early secondary school visual education.

A good deal of research has been published in the last few years which aims to establish scientifically what was probably known all along, but had become buried under the excesses of the child-centred approach: namely, that children can and do develop through a sequence of stages in their ability to receive, articulate, appraise and form judgements about works of visual art. It would, of course, be highly surprising if this were not so. All the same, the precise description of these stages, perhaps even the measurement of them, has become a field which is ripe for experiment and rich in implications for the art educational fraternity. A recent major study by Parsons, Johnston and Durham in the United States, for example [1], pointed convincingly to six discrete topics which contained developmental levels; *semblance* (whether and how a painting refers); *subject-matter* (what paintings refer to); *feelings* (the affect *in* the painting); *colour* (what colours are most pleasing); *properties of the artist* (the requirements of artistry); and *judgement* (reasons for aesthetic judgements). We know merely from everyday living that children change their responses along all of these dimensions as they grow and mature. What the study hinted at, however, but did not state, was that teachers could use this information in planning the contents of art appreciation lessons—in order to intensify, perhaps even accelerate, the pleasures and rewards of art at each developmental stage.

It actually matters little for our purposes whether the number of developmental topics in the Parsons study was six or sixty; or whether the number of developmental levels is three (as the authors state) or thirty-three. What matters is the assumptions upon which the experiment was based, the kind of teaching towards which it is implicitly aimed. A striking aspect of this type of survey for example is the *range* of images used. An assumption made by the Parsons study was to use—with perhaps one exception—canonical works of the modern tradition, that is, avant-garde art from about 1850. Thus a *Head of a Man* by Klee; Picasso's *Weeping Woman* of 1932; and Renoir's *Girl and a Dog* for the ages roughly 5 to 11; and then Picasso's *Guernica*, one of Marc Chagall's *Circus* pictures, and Bellow's *Dempsey and Firpo* for the ages roughly 12 to 17. No reasons were given in the Parsons study either for the choice of images or for the distinction between the two age-groups; but I think we can speculate on the reasons and justifications for the choice. There are two factors here which deserve analysis: one is the assumption of the 'goodness' of 'high art'; and the other, already mentioned, is the 'goodness' of modernity.

First, the distinction between high or museum art and other types of visual imagery such as posters, television imagery, street signs and book illustrations is one that carries with it several assumptions about the 'creativity' and 'insight' of the artist, and about the special status of his work. Now frankly I do not know whether or not such assumptions can be upheld. Even if they can, it is surely questionable whether such assumptions should be made implicitly, without announcement to the young and thus far innocent audience. In any case, the assumption of a hard and fast dividing line between art and the remainder of the world's manufactured imagery seems to me not at all helpful at this very early stage.

Secondly, the presentation to young children of 'high art' images which are ready to hand in large numbers at an economic price is an activity which is, of necessity, both value-laden and highly selective. The inescapable fact is that only a minute fraction of the world's output of visual images is available in reproduction for mass circulation to schools, colleges and art education seminars, any yet this fact continues to go unnoticed by the majority of both producers and consumers of juvenile education in art. Indeed, this type of pedagogy may conceal more than is revealed by the pictures themselves. For instance, it seems to me to conceal the fact that 'high art' is unpopular with all but the middle or educated classes. It implicitly short-cuts the possibility that the children might value these images not at all, or even negatively. It certainly conceals the present-day use of these artworks—many of them produced without thought of a sale-price—as blue chip investments for the extremely rich; and finally it seems to me to reproduce and perpetuate a value-ranking of visual images which is often one devised by the museum for the purpose of maximising a sense of 'heritage' in the country concerned, and for heightening sales to tourists. I think one simply has to face the fact that an innocent-looking experiment in art education comes hand-in-hand, inexorably and inevitably, with a ready-made ideology of art and art production whose real nature is completely concealed.

An over-arching problem here is that any image shown without judgement to a class of children is liable, unless a disclaimer is made, to be seen by them not merely as meeting with the teacher's personal approval, but as indicative of adult taste in general. That there may be no way of presenting images value-free, without an implicit *imprimatur* from the adult world, should constitute a definite *problem* in visual education (not merely in art but in literature and history) at this early level.

A secondary problem, vastly exacerbated by the current restraints on teachers' pay and resources in the United Kingdom, is that the reduction of an artwork to the size and scale of a postcard encourages a 'reading' of the artefact which is not necessarily compatible with its intended or received purpose. Placed in a horizontal plane for easy inspection, it becomes suddenly a specimen to be copied, turned upside down, written across or sent through the post; while the artwork's luminosity, volume (in the case of sculpture), and 'thingness' all but disappear in the process. This substitution of art by an inexpensive piece of printed card conceals almost entirely the *made* quality of the object—its identity as a crafted as opposed to a mechanically reproduced thing.

But these are general difficulties. The problem of modernity—the why and the how of presenting modernity in the classroom—is I believe more specific and at the same time more difficult to discuss. I have mentioned already the fact that all six of Parsons' images were drawn from the modern period; granting for purposes of the argument that Renoir and Bellows are both modern. Now certainly it cannot be claimed, even by the wildest stretching of the facts, that modern art of the generation of Picasso, Chagall and Klee was produced for the consumption of children, even if the inspiration of children's art was a formative factor in certain of these artists, in Klee in particular and to a lesser degree in the others. I think the main problem here for teachers is to recognise the very *peculiarity* and *specificity* of modern culture.

Art teachers will be aware that modern art—the term is at once contentious and contested—came into being in circumstances which are both extraordinary but also historically specific. Denoting nothing so simple as a stylistic 'development', modernity in painting and sculpture announced itself sometime in the course of the nineteenth century, partly as a symptom of shifting class identifications, partly as a vogue for contemporaneity, partly as a response to the changing inner life of the individual under conditions of developing capitalism. Certainly the aetiology, and to that extent the meaning, of modernism is a complex but also a controversial topic, of high relevance, one would think, to the education of the young adult—but scarcely suitable for the younger child. For the nature of this art as both ideology and history is impossible to dissociate from the visual data as given. It should be impossible to separate the social and cultural formations surrounding Picasso's Blue Period pictures—which I mention here only because of their frequent use in the classroom—from the images themselves, his sense of exile in Paris after 1901 and his response to the urban poverty by which he was suddenly surrounded.

By the time of Cubism and Expressionism—also popular but only vaguely understood examples of early twentieth century Modernism—the concept of avant-garde or oppositional art had become firmly entrenched as a viable alternative aesthetic, both in the studios but particularly in the salerooms, as an antidote to, or critique of, bourgeois urban life. The wilful experimentalism, the wild distortions, the unfinished surfaces, were registered by the bourgeois public of 1912 or 1914 as something more serious than a play of form and technique in unfamiliar styles. The displaced optic of so-called academic art had for generations been an adequate vehicle for a coherent set of moral, ultimately political convictions, grounded in economic order, rational choice, in commodification and in the possession by an ailing capitalist tradition of its own goods, services and history. Avant-garde or oppositional art entered the market place as a foil to this declining moral order: colourful, distracted, anti-technical but highly liberated in its appearances. Its characteristic freedoms—its distortions, fragmentations and explicit displays of paint as worked substance—these novelties were received by the bourgeoisie as constituting a kind of limitation on its presumed capacity for endless erotic, domestic or rustic fantasy; a kind of limitation on its taste for illusions of history, or for anecdote. My complaints against the use of modernistic images in the school classroom revolve precisely therefore around the fact that almost nothing of this wider context can hope to

103

enter the running alongside the power of the unadorned image to communicate itself merely as colour, shape and texture. And yet I suspect that no teacher of primary or secondary children would dream of introducing Joyce, Apollinaire or Proust into the classroom as con-figurations of sound and pattern alone.

The question is simply whether the reduction of modern art to the level of the visually 'given' is desirable. My argument already will have indicated a major difficulty, perhaps even an insuperable one. But there is a further complication. It is evident from virtually every 'cognitive-developmental' study of childhood art appreciation that during the years of progressive accumulation of technical skill in representational drawing the child will baulk, apparently instinctively, at the modern expressively distorted picture. Before the age of perhaps 12 or 13—I tread carefully here for fear of simplification—a typical response to the situation is simply that all distortions are bad. The ages between 5 and 15 elicit this verdict in varying degrees, ranging from the child who will assert without qualification that the painting is 'bad' or 'amateur' to the verdict that you 'can't tell what it is' [2], to the more discriminating response which accepts the buckled fingers in Picasso's *Weeping Woman* (1932) but baulks at the eyes which are both positioned on the same side of the face. A study published in 1983 indicated the same [3]. Children confronted with even so mild a transformation as Derain's *Pool of London* (1906, Tate Gallery) were unanimous in judging the picture to be 'poor' and the artist only an 'amateur'.

In some ways the child's difficulty with the concept of modern ex-pressive distortion is entirely to be expected, given his acculturation. On the one hand, children inherit aesthetic attitudes from their parents' reactions to photography, snapshots especially—and we know that a belief in verisimilitude is taken for granted by the majority of the popu-lation. A photograph which is blurred in any part, for example, is *ipso facto* bad. One which catches a friend in an off-guard moment—sneezing, blinking or glancing away—is appraised automatically as an inferior representation, however much it might show the truth of the moment. Television pictures which show an actor or newscaster fluffing his lines or mincing his words will attract derisory laughter since the assumed norm of 'how things should be' has been—however acciden-tally—contravened. Fun-fair mirrors which distort the human figure are also hilarious because they falsify what is felt to be real and true. Thus the general hostility to modern art which is endemic in the majority of the adult population will already have been transmitted to the child of 5 or 6 and upwards, if I am right, alongside other widely shared cultural norms of our society. Modern painting which appears to distort reality has an immense task to perform if it is to persuade the viewer—however young—that distortion is in some sense an aid to truth (as modern artists have often claimed) rather than its enemy.

It is reasonable to assume therefore that despite its popularity with museum curators and despite its interest to historians, modern art has had little or no purchase on the optic of restrained naturalism that still dominates the tastes of the population as a whole. To study modern art

104

in the classroom is therefore to come up against the barriers that have been erected against it—for better or worse—in the population at large. And it would seem to follow from this that to confront these barriers actively through the planned discussion of modern art in the classroom requires a real belief on the part of the teacher that Modernism represents something other than a specialist minority programme in artistic culture with a special, and frequently perplexing (though not perhaps finally unintelligible) structure; that it represents, perhaps, a moment of supposed 'liberation' or 'progress' to which all people irrespective of age or education can gain access. Perhaps some teachers genuinely have this belief—but I doubt whether, once acknowledged, it could remain unchallenged for long.

But the barriers are not all cultural. In fact I believe there is an over-arching psychological reason, perhaps even a biological one, why young people are averse to modern pictures unless countervailing attractions are called into play. One factor which may determine a child's hostility to extreme expressive distortion is that, during the years up to and even beyond puberty, the child is learning to represent the world (both to himself and to others) as it actually and optically *is*. The matter is of course controversial—but it would appear that, to some extent, standards of representational 'accuracy' are simply *there*, as given and recognisable data—present in community-wide assumptions about how close a drawing (or other representation) comes to its object. This is a large proposition, admittedly, and it is intended to imply no allegiance to any particular form of Realist art. Rather, the point is to argue that a well-understood critique of the basically naturalistic mode may involve a far higher level of conceptualisation than is available to the pre-pubescent child.

Second, the level of toleration the child possesses for painfully frag-mented images is necessarily lower than that of the adult—and long may it remain so. As can be easily verified, the violence unleashed upon natural appearances by a 'cubified' representation or an Expressionist caricature can—I repeat can—appear deeply threatening and disturbing to a mind unequipped to cope with adult sophistications. The similarity between Picasso's high Cubist portraits and the appearances of imaginary demons or somehow violated presences should act as a caution to those who might suppose a knowledge of Cubism to be 'beneficial' to minors. Equally, of course, some distortions can be highly exciting to children. The point is not to consign the whole category to off-limits, but to point to the existence of a threshold.

Thus I believe the approach taken by Tony Dyson in Chapter 11 is naïve in this respect. Recognising all too clearly the perplexity induced in his young audience by the distortions of the Cubist portrait, Tony Dyson advises that

> the formal principle of distortion (among other important
> characteristics) will need to be appraised, explored and understood
> by pupils.

I personally cannot imagine what childhood 'need' could be satisfied by understanding such a thing. In any case, Dyson omits to mention that

that which he calls the 'formal principle of distortion' probably does not exist as a unified method of image-making, capable of being copied by several artists at once; for in fact different practices of distortion are to be found in different artists at different times. Nor does he recognise the fact that distortion in any of its particular forms is one of the most obscure and difficult topics in the whole of modern aesthetic thought, and its application to Cubist art is a particularly baffling subject upon which little has been written and probably even less understood. But he goes even further. He proposes, and here I quote in full, that

> such explorations will profitably include a consideration of examples within the scope of pupils' existing interests and experience— examples which need have no link with art beyond the fact that they happen to be illustrative of the particular principle or principles under consideration. The vital property of such examples will be their capacity to bridge pupils' existing awareness and their ultimate understanding of particular art objects.

I seriously doubt whether any such 'bridging' devices exist. Nor will it do, I fear, to attempt to round out the teaching with historical information about the aims and purposes of Cubism, obscure as these still are even to professional historians. Collateral information about the artist's intentions is not always easy to find; and, in the case of the modern picture and particularly the Cubist one, extremely difficult if not impossible to convey to an audience lacking a considerable degree of cultural and historical awareness. In short, I remain sceptical whether the intricacies of Cubist portraiture can be sensibly addressed by the mind of a 7 or a 10 or a 13-year-old school-child at all. And in any case, what counts as 'understanding'?

The point can be made equally strongly for the case of abstract art. I have seen children of a very young age—perhaps as young as 8 or 9— presented with postcards of the highly 'popular' pre-war Kandinskys and invited to respond to them in terms of colour-appreciation, skill, and subject-identification. The fact that these images are available in postcard form is, as mentioned already, a peculiar cultural fact all by itself—one with its own specific causation and historical meaning which would certainly repay investigation. Here, it is reasonable to assume that the children themselves, unable to travel to New York or Hamburg to see the paintings at first hand, will be led to a set of ideas about Kandinsky's picture which probably mirrors the teacher's own. These are: that the painting is basically a pattern of bright shapes and colours; that it does not matter which way up the painting stands; that it is one of the first 'abstract' pictures in modern art; that it involved relatively little skill but a high premium of intuition; that some of the shapes can probably be read as 'fishes', 'the sun', 'the sea' and so forth—identifications which the teacher regards as secondary to the meaning of the picture as a whole.

It seems to me that the enormous dangers in this process—and obviously I caricature the actual situation considerably here—is that the child will learn and retain what is, in effect, a completely false view of Kandinsky and his work as a basically trivial but pleasing artist who, like

106

34   WASSILY KANDINSKY *Traümerische Improvisation*, 1913, oil on canvas 51·25
× 51·25″; Städtische Galerie im Lenbachhaus, München, © ADAGP,
Paris & DACS, London, 1989.

35, 36   Children's copies (1985) of postcard reproductions of a KANDINSKY
Traümerische Improvisation.
(photos: Taylor, B)

other early abstractionists, aimed principally at entertaining the viewer with the brightness of his colours and the playfulness of his forms—but little more.

I suspect that the scenario I have just caricatured may be familiar to many an art teacher today. That Kandinsky was deeply immersed in pre-First World War mysticism; that his friends in Munich's bohemian suburb, many of them health-food zealots and world-reforming priests, would be considered highly eccentric if their views were to be expressed today; that Kandinsky himself was a wealthy and highly educated Russian academic who adopted the contemporary concern for world-apocalypse and spiritual reform; that at the time of the painting he may have been close to breakdown, perhaps even in the middle of an identity crisis; that he experienced synaesthesia; that the 'abstract' pictures were highly unspontaneous, even laboured; that Kandinsky could not draw; that he wanted his art to mirror the world crisis which he believed was about to come; and that his art was attractive mainly to 'modern' dealers who supplied a wealthy intellectual middle class. *These* sorts of facts, which are capable of transforming a highly coloured postcard image into a rich, even if somewhat puzzling, historical document about a unique period in a small corner of early twentieth century cultural life—these facts, of necessity, are liable to remain remote from the teaching of young children of the primary age. Indeed I would here argue what I proposed for the Cubist portrait—that a seriously wrong understanding is worse than no understanding at all—and counsel extreme caution generally in making assumptions about the relevance of early twentieth century avant-garde art images to the life and developing interests of the younger child.

What warnings might be given for the case of the Old Masters? Here, the attractions of ready-made colour reproductions of pictures of high notoriety, such as Constable's *Haywain*, Leonardo's *Mona Lisa* or Géricault's *The Raft of the Medusa*, are similar to those offered by reproductions of modern paintings; and the dangers correspond. The difficulties which stem from modern art's peculiar and unique character —its oppositional nature, its freedoms and distortions—are happily missing; but the problem of representing for the child something of the unique ideological, social and psychological meaning of particular Old Master images surely remains.

The difficulties became visible for me during an experiment in which 6-year-olds were invited to 'copy' two pictures—Raphael's *Virgin and Child Enthroned with Saints John the Baptist and Nicholas of Bari* (the Ansidei altarpiece of 1505, now in the National Gallery, London); and Millet's *Gleaners* of 1857. Here, the children reacted to the small postcard placed before them rather than to the painting itself, as before. The postcard miniaturised the picture to the point where it could be perceived whole, as a *Gestalt*, and, when placed in the same plane as the child's own work, lent itself well to the process of transcription. In some ways therefore it was not surprising that the painting was perceived as pattern, and only secondarily in terms of human or religious drama. The broad arch over the four figures in the Raphael, the symmetry of the group, the block-like architecture of the Virgin's throne—these features

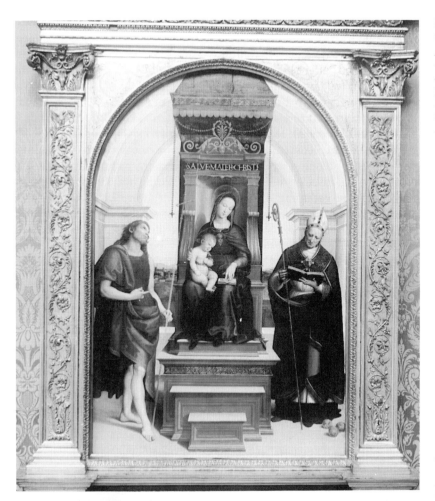

37 RAPHAEL *Virgin and Child Enthroned with saints John the Baptist and Nicholas of Bari (The Ansidei Altarpiece),* 1506–7, oil on panel 107·9 × 59·8"; National Gallery, London. (photo: Bridgeman Art Library)

38, 39 Children's copies (1985) of RAPHAEL'S *Virgin and Child Enthroned with Saints John the Baptist and Nicholas of Bari.* (photos: Taylor, B)

were noticed and reproduced *within* the child's already existent ability to render arrangement and visual form The figures themselves were seldom identified correctly. John the Baptist and St Nicholas of Bari are beyond the experience of most 6-year-olds; while the Virgin and Child were instantly perceived not in terms of Biblical lore but in terms of the universal biological relationship of mother and child. (That the infant is being read a bedtime story was a favourite response to the scene.)

Responses to the Millet postcard necessarily involved obliterating any reference to the economic or social status of the gleaners themselves, depicting the stooping women simply in terms of picking up corn. The events in the distance of the picture, including the supervisor on his horse and the gathering of the harvest itself, were in this case barely visible in a small reproduction—certainly not capable of being registered as a kind of counterpart to the situation of the gleaners. Once again, it is the painting *as an historical image* that becomes a casualty in the process of merely 'copying' or 'reacting to' the postcard version of a work of art.

40   JEAN-FRANCOIS MILLET *The Gleaners*, 1857, oil on canvas 33 × 44"; Louvre, Paris. (photo: Lauros/ Giraudon. Bridgeman)

41, 42   Children's copies (1985) of MILLET'S *The Gleaners*.
(photos: Taylor, B)

111

The trouble, of course, is that in one sense the results of such experiments are remarkable. They startle and delight us in ways which other examples of children's artistry do not. We marvel at the child's struggle to come to terms successfully with Old Master paintings and we can enjoy the child's absorption—often unexpectedly long—in a task with which he or she is so obviously unfamiliar. But our pleasure in the child's achievement is surely capable of bearing examination, however tentative. Do we not find the process endearing—'charming' is again perhaps the word—because of the very gulf between the virtuosity of the Raphael and the artlessness of the child? Are we not being entertained by the very transformation which a child has wrought in converting a deeply venerated icon into a merely colourful diagram? And is not our sense of heightened achievement, finally, to be attributed chiefly to a sense of having made a connection between the realm of adult culture and the world of the child?

That these pleasures may ultimately be illusory is the danger that we must confront. Contact with the values of early sixteenth century Italian culture, or those of the nineteenth century French, is precluded precisely by what we do *not* convey to the child about the task to which he or she has been put. Any grasp of the material nature of the artefact is, of course, utterly denied. The very scale, construction and physical presence of such pictures cannot be conveyed in words and is, I think, best not attempted. The rootedness of artistic production in the values of the market place—Raphael's financial interests in the picture, or Millet's in his—cannot be broached to a child who has not yet grasped the basic facts of monetary exchange. The influence of the commissioner (in Raphael's case the role of Bernadino Ansidei himself) must inevitably be left aside. The history of the picture, its cycles of veneration and neglect at the hands of subsequent generations, must also be necessarily omitted, even in outline form, before the age at which the child can give such information a place within his own developing understanding. In short, it may have to be faced that art history *cannot* be simplified to the level of 7 or 9-year-old comprehension in the way that arithmetic or the rudiments of reading can. If this is indeed the case, then it follows that a child's first steps in art-historical understanding may have to wait until a sufficient groundwork in other disciplines such as history and sociology—and pre-eminently the practice of art itself—has already been provided.

References

1   PARSONS, M., M JOHNSTON and R DURHAM. 1978. Developmental Stages in Children's Aesthetic Responses, *Journal of Aesthetic Education*, Vol. 12, No. 1.
2   *Ibid.* p. 88.
3   TURNER, P. 1983. Children's Responses to Art: Interpretation and Criticism, *Journal of Art and Design Education*, Vol. 2, No. 2.

Chapter Ten

MAUREEN PRICE Art History and Critical Studies in Schools: an Inclusive Approach

My general intention is to argue that the acquisition of critical skills should be an essential objective in the education of each and every pupil, and that within the broad spectrum of the visual arts there is enormous potential for providing the means to develop the individual's critical powers. In particular, I maintain strong commitment to the feasibility of taught access to the artistic production of any and all specific periods or cultures. This raises a point of contention, however, for the notion of an *Art History and Critical Studies* programme that is at once comprehensive and thorough is considered unrealistic by at least one other contributor to this volume [1]. My primary objective, then, is to review and, I hope, expand upon present attitudes to broad access courses, and to consider the types of teaching programmes which are most appropriate to their aims. First, though, there is a need, made urgent by current proposals for educational restructuring, to question certain assumptions about the character and status of the subject.

For almost two decades the academic foundations of art historical study have been challenged by a significant body of opinion seeking to broaden the base of the subject. This shifting perspective entails a concern for a more diversified range of cultural products, examining the conditions of production and consumption within the widest context. Many of the ideas that have contributed to this change of emphasis, now filtering into the mainstream, have emanated from 'non-academic' disciplines such as film and media studies. These same disciplines have, in recent years, been introduced into the secondary school curriculum to form a basis for contemporary studies, expanding the premises of traditional English teaching. This has provided valuable experience in the rudiments of critical debate for a wide range of pupils, including many disaffected with more orthodox pedagogy. Simultaneously, an importance has become attached to the inclusion of *Art History and Critical Studies* within art and design education. Those educationists who have pressed for this have been aware of current discourses in art history, have sought to extend the parameters of the subjects in schools, and have tried to do this taking account of the range of abilities, aptitudes and socio-cultural experiences of their pupils. The hope is that by radically extending the dimensions of traditional course content, there can be far greater participation in the discussion of issues relevant to the cultural heritage of every child.

In many respects these objectives are compatible with the educational ethics at the basis of the new GCSE art and design courses, and a number

113

of exemplary schemes are well-established [2]. However, my initial concern here is to concentrate on the methodological problems involved at the incipient, preparatory stages of teaching this subject. This is a crucial area for consideration, not merely because the success of the subject will be highly dependent upon its quality, but more significantly because the actual viability of the subject area itself may be at stake in the present climate of educational reform towards 'core curriculum' subjects. Therefore, whilst it is unfortunate that defensive rhetoric still needs to be employed, it must be acknowledged that convincing and clearly-stated principles must yet be registered as being of elementary educational value, and that rationalised though not prescriptive teaching strategies must accordingly be proposed.

It is precisely for these reasons that analogies need to be made between the inherent principles and methods of *Art History and Critical Studies* and those of other subjects which are accorded greater status within current conceptions of a 'core curriculum'. It need not be assumed, for example, that other, more favoured subjects, are distinguishable from it in any of the following respects—in their potential for methodological rationalisation; in their facility for the systematic transmittance of skills; in their embrace of problematical bodies of knowledge; in their addressing of conflicting ideological values; in their opportunities for opposing entrenched notions with some degree of revisionism; in the richness of their potential for the development of the logical faculties; or in the fundamentality of their relevance to daily experience.

No such assumptions are accepted here. Instead I argue positively that the type of *Art History and Critical Studies* course that I envisage—one that seeks to encourage a penetrating analysis of visual imagery, and the examination of cultural artefacts within the broadest psychological, social, economic and ideological context—is undoubtedly equal in value to any 'core' subject in terms of the essential nature of the conceptual skills it seeks to develop. Furthermore, I believe that the difficulties of devising introductory courses for this subject area are neither more nor less problematic than those encountered elsewhere in the curriculum. As in other areas of knowledge, a complex body of ideas has to be transmitted by a gradual process without recourse to reductionism or misrepresentation. This is our challenge; and the following remarks are addressed to possible responses.

It must be acknowledged that there has been much unenlightened teaching of *Art History and Critical Studies*. Ill-formulated and unsubstantiated opinions have often been conveyed to pupils, in substitution for the sound critical vocabulary needed to form the basis of later, personal investigation. Given that it is the development of critical skills as a means towards proper understanding, and not the imposition of opinionated rhetoric, which should be the prime objective of our discipline, then certain fundamental questions need to be addressed. What are the elementary tools of art historical criticism? What does an appropriate critical vocabulary consist of? And what is its point of access?

A document published in 1988 by the London and East Anglia Group for GCSE Examinations [3] coherently states the aims of its *Critical Studies in Art and Design (GCSE 'Mature')* course, and these conform to the National General Criteria. Its objectives, summarised, consist of the development of the skills of 'accurate description, clear analysis and thoughtful interpretation', leading to the ability to make independent judgements, offer reasoned arguments and identify significant issues in the discussion and presentation of art historical material. My immediate interest, however, is to identify the specific type of activity that constitutes the development of such study skills, and which may thereby claim to provide initial access to the cultural heritage.

Whilst it is the aim of art historical enquiry to proceed far beyond the visually given, it is nevertheless the expression of spontaneous and unrationalised reactions to the visually given that will initiate discussion. Subjective and empirical responses, stated without inhibition, serve to raise a perplexity of attitudes, expectations and feelings which will need to be clarified, thus leading to the consideration of meanings within the image. Since there can be no finite or non-contradictory account of meaning within a representation, then the aim must be to introduce the pupil to some of the multifarious processes at work within the production of meaning.

In this there can be no *single* approach, since the particular methods employed will be determined by a *range* of possible objectives. Therefore, while suggesting here that the consideration of formal representational structures may constitute an area for early discussion, I recognise that this is but one possibility. But it is one which, in the context of current classroom activity, may be regarded as being most useful to build upon the relatively limited experiences of the pupil, and as such it does, perhaps, provide a more readily accessible route towards participation in the complex language of an art historical debate.

The pupil does not necessarily need an awareness of the rudiments of formal composition, or of material qualities, in order to express affection or loathing for a particular visual image. But he or she will keenly require an understanding of the formal mechanisms operative within the work if the personal response is to be more precisely and effectively articulated. This is already to suggest to the pupil that formal and material qualities are integrated carriers of meaning. It should not be seen to imply that formal criteria embody autonomous values, or that they represent a single analytical tool which may be used in isolation from a network of others.

Nothing can be gained from a reluctance to engage the issue of formal criteria. Indeed, the lack of attention to a concise formal analysis may constitute a serious weakness in any contextualised art historical enquiry. Dissatisfaction with the Modernist paradigm, with its theory of autonomous values and 'disinterested art', has understandably created anxiety amongst many art historians, and some may wish to de-emphasise the formal aspect of artistic debate for fear of encouraging false or incomplete readings. However, a recognition of the strengths and limitations of the Modernist approach can only be legitimised through a familiarity with its ideas, and also with the oppositional arguments, and this in turn will depend on a precise knowledge of a formal vocabulary.

Formal analysis of the visually given must therefore be permitted to serve as an entry point to that which otherwise risks being inaccessible. The important factor is to ensure that it is done well, and it is in this direction that energies need to be concentrated.

A familiarity with the basic formal elements of compositional design is a teachable asset that can be developed from an early stage. A combination of perceptual and expressive skills is employed in the development of visual discrimination, so that any programme must proceed by degrees by means of the practice of combined verbal and artistic skills, involving the manipulation of ideas and materials, towards abilities to make increasingly refined identifications and classifications. The importance of relative, and not of absolute, values needs to be accentuated throughout the learning process. Encouragement of critical appraisal is increased in value and relevance by direct reference to a range of appropriate artistic and cultural products, but it needs constantly to be stated that formal criteria *alone* will not determine the quality or meaning of such works. Contextual factors, which may have contributed to the final forms of such works, will need to be recognised. Sound judgement in both the selection of artefacts and the perception of the pupil's level of comprehension, is therefore essential.

As a possible point of access, the discussion model proposed by Tony Dyson in Chapter 11, for the structuring of early art historical study, contains some useful ideas, but I wish to suggest certain notes of caution. Grounded in techniques of systematic comparison of visual images, Dyson's approach could stimulate a level of discussion based on careful observation of the visually given, but encouraging the practice of reading 'from' rather than 'into' images. There can be no pretence, however, (as Dyson himself undoubtedly recognises) that such an exercise can engage with the wider cultural implications of formal criteria. Accordingly it is possible to attempt basic classifications, such as Dyson's 'verticality-horizontality' and 'lightness-darkness', provided these are considered as both contingent and relative, and not definitive, values.

In so far as Dyson recommends the use of postcard reproductions for the sake of classroom convenience, it must be recognised that the types of possible classification are fairly restricted. In particular, it needs to be made explicit to the pupil that where the postcard print reproduces a cultural artefact, it inevitably results in serious misrepresentation. However, this does not invalidate its use in classification exercises *per se*, since it permits a degree of analysis to take place, albeit within the specific constraints of a peculiar and highly standardised format. As such, where its use is occasional and complements the direct experience of actual works, the use of postcard reproductions is an admissible activity.

A more pressing concern arises from the further evaluation of other formal polarities suggested by Dyson. For example, 'obscurity-definition' and 'depth-flatness' are somewhat loaded terms in post-Modernist discussion. It may be foreseen that the finer distinctions and contradictions perceived by the initiated, and the particular need here for acute sensibility in the selection of images for discussion, would not be recognised by the non-specialist teacher. However, even here where the mutability of the terminology has been stressed, there need be no impairment of educational effectiveness. It should not be necessary, on grounds of intellectual complexity *for either teacher or pupil*, to eliminate categories of images or entire epochs of artistic production from any stage of the pupil's development.

The artistic production of every epoch and region must be equally regarded as historically and culturally specific. No single area of cultural production should be regarded as more uniquely complex in its innate character, or more easily 'de-codable' and fully understandable, either within its own context or in its subsequent reception into another. Obviously, it would be naïve and arrogant to assume that the distancing effects of time or place render areas of cultural production less problematic in terms of the recovery of their meanings. Conversely, the much theorised and abundantly documented recent artistic activity of our own specific culture, whilst explicitly laying claim to a 'difficult' intellectualism, may be no more conceptually unfathomable than that of other eras.

Accessibility needs to be accepted as a problem equally applicable to the study of all cases. Having stated this I must acknowledge the enormity of the challenge now facing schools that are ambitiously attempting to address a vast range of cultural production by means of contextualised study. These schools, or rather their teachers, need to be more fully supported, in terms of rhetoric and material resources, by all those professional agencies with a responsible concern. I have referred to possible points of access to a critical language, but subsequent development beyond access may depend, to a large extent, upon the types of attitude encountered in agencies outside the schools themselves.

For example, the manner in which public and private collections are exhibited and made accessible has an important bearing on this problem. Given that such institutions are in the first place willing to make their collections widely accessible (which is not always evident), their advantages over the school environment oblige them to raise certain types of open-ended questions, not always possible with reproductions, about the artefacts that they present. An enlightened attitude towards display can offer insights into the wider conditions of original production, and provoke consideration of a variety of relationships within that process, in a manner that the classroom, of course, cannot rival.

Also required in the construction of an enabling support system for *Art History and Critical Studies* are the publishers and writers of art historical literature, little of which is currently aimed below the undergraduate market. By refraining *en masse* from addressing the specialist needs of the younger reader, they are seriously failing to meet the demands of schools. Much is written about art history in schools: precious little is written for it. This neglect exacerbates existing problems of under-resourced departments, and perpetuates a sense of low esteem which pervades the subject area in the lower sectors of the educational system. Professional art historians, 'new' and otherwise, have generally failed to take the initiative here.

Many of those involved in the writing of art historical material are also instrumental in the organisation of teaching programmes in higher education. Yet, despite the enthusiasm for newer approaches to the subject in polytechnics and universities, and the obvious links they might have with *Art History and Critical Studies* courses in schools, no significant connections have been fostered to encourage the discussion of common pedagogical concerns. It may be that this is because, despite the vociferous concerns for methodology in the tertiary sector, there is perhaps less analysis of, and accountability for, the development of study skills here than in schools. In the secondary, and most emphatically in the primary, sectors the acquisition of knowledge and the development of study skills are seen as inextricably linked. These are often taken as prerequisites by the tertiary sector, and this places unfair burdens on the lower sectors, and especially upon art history teaching in their institutions, staffed as this subject is by relatively few specialists. In effect this sustains the *status quo*, wherein knowledge remains the preserve of higher education while identification of the learning process remains the problem of the schools. The lack of a more united commitment to resolving this disparity can only have a damaging effect on the matter of wider accessibility.

In this respect the recommendations of Brandon Taylor, published here in Chapter 9, carry disturbing implications, for he concludes that certain of the problems that arise in the teaching of art history in schools are insurmountable. Taylor, an art historian working in the tertiary sector, surveys the gamut of difficulties likely to be encountered in primary education, and concludes that modern abstract art constitutes a minority culture that is frequently inappropriate, technically and emotionally, for presentation to the growing child. Images of a different order must form the basis of early education.

I have already emphasised the need for a sensitive and rationalised approach to the selection of visual imagery. But I question Taylor's hypothesis that a specific area of cultural production may constitute a special category, beyond the range of educational competence provided by the classroom study skills of *Art History and Critical Studies* in primary or early secondary schooling.

Taylor's main contention is that the conceptual powers of the child will not be sufficiently developed to enable a full understanding of the complexities of meaning within the imagery of twentieth century western avant-garde art, with its characteristic use of formal abstraction. He fears that pupils will be unable to conceive of the works in question as anything other than configurations of colour, shape, and texture, or that at most they will be variously excited or traumatised by their confrontation with formally-distorted appearances. Noting the majority preference for versimilitude, he suggests the intervention of 'natural', psychological, and cultural barriers to the acceptance of distorted imagery 'unless countervailing attractions are called into play'.

It is my contention that counterbalancing factors can of course be introduced if necessary. It should be borne in mind that formal distortion is common to much pre-Renaissance European art, and is employed

118

quite radically in the art of other cultures. As such, it pervades much of the art pertinent to discussion in the multi-cultural classroom. In this respect, then, Modernism is not so distinct from other artistic traditions, and its propensity for signification through the use of formal distortion is not necessarily richer, nor more problematic, than these.

There is a strong likelihood that any aversion to such formal distortion, far from being instinctive, is a 'schooled' reaction; yet it is fortunately the case that pupils often respond enthusiastically to the appearances of certain types of formal abstraction and fragmentation, especially in the context of their own practical artwork. This is not without explanation, for such forms have been widely appropriated within mass culture, and children are familiar with their presence in the graphic art forms of comics, advertising, and fashion photography, as well as in 'pop' videos. More correctly, this amounts to misappropriation, a popular misusage of the established forms of avant-garde art, which has largely involved an uncritical approach to the original sources. Yet as a cultural phenomenon this is not unconnected to past practices, and this could provide a singularly useful point of access for *Art History and Critical Studies.*

For instance, Richard Cork has described an earlier example of the popular trivialisation of contemporary art practice, as Italian Futurism made its impact on Britain before the First World War [4]. He describes how the press and the advertising industry went into full operation, adding to the furore created by the paintings themselves and the presence of Marinetti. Consequently, the name 'Futurist' was arbitrarily ascribed to anything marketed as 'new', ranging from men's pyjamas to interior decoration schemes. Simultaneously, Cork continues, the true concerns of Futurist painting remained a mystery to the public at large.

There are many other instances of this phenomenon within twentieth century cultural practice, which surely constitutes a relevant issue for class discussion, for the relationship between 'mass' and 'minority' culture should not be considered insignificant to the school population. A recognition of the ways in which specialist artistic practice, however misappropriated, may enter the public consciousness, and, more specifically, their own culture, may for some pupils provide the only worthwhile reason for looking at original artefacts at all. It is to be hoped that this will suggest to them a direction for further study, and so hinder to some extent the processes that perpetuate the widespread ignorance of art among the general population.

The type of activity that aims to explore such links might lead to a more thorough investigation and appreciation of the specific historical and cultural conditions in which the relevant artistic practices originally occurred. This in turn has the potential to reveal the superficiality of apparent similarities in the visual appearances of cultural products emanating from different realms or epochs, encouraging in pupils a recognition of diverse interests and meanings within the works. The value of a discriminating and investigative approach to the visually given can be suggested through such comparisons.

There is a positive factor in an exercise of this kind, which attempts

119

to begin from a starting point in the culture already familiar to most pupils. It has the advantage of building upon the pupil's predisposition towards some types of formally distorted imagery, a tolerance that derives from the subconscious acceptance of such forms as visual metaphors for modernity. This at least provides a basis for the questioning of some popular misconceptions about formal abstraction, and an opportunity for the acquisition of knowledge, and the development of a fuller understanding of the kinds of issues which have determined the nature of such forms. It will be the case that any such discussions will remain limited in scope in accordance with the present learning capacity of the pupil; but the necessary and temporary simplifications can also be well-formulated, and need not be trivialised.

When formal distortion is least acceptable to the pupil, it appears to be rejected on the basis of a perceived lack of artistic skill. The prejudices and misconceptions are particularly complex here for, predictably, the predominant Eurocentric attitude dictates that although an artefact which is perceived to be of ethnological character, or of ancient origin, might be excused for its inevitable 'crudity' of technique or 'primitivism' of form, the same qualities are likely to be despised in artefacts produced more recently in the indigenous culture. There is no doubt that such disturbing preconceptions about the notions of skill, value, quality and meaning in art, as well as the concomitant, conditioned attitudes to 'civilisation', present a daunting problem that requires delicate management. But where the pupil's prejudices are strongly held, they may also be loudly voiced, and penetrating questions may be posed, demanding a response. Such queries sometimes arise from events outside the classroom—for example, from media coverage of record auction prices for modern paintings. Since pupils themselves may well raise such problem issues, there can be no ambiguity of stance from educationists. It might also be considered that, where multicultural concerns are an educational priority, the racially-mixed class provides a positively advantaged position from which to confront responsibly such problematical issues in the art of different cultures.

Any programme that aims to enable pupils to adopt more open and informed attitudes to the range of appearances and possible meanings of formal distortion, or in any other aspect of visual representation, will somehow have to make explicit its central premise that academic canons of form and the Renaissance system of linear perspective, which have been constructive to European notions of versimilitude, themselves constitute distortions of reality. Though rich in its connotations, this is not a straightforward concept to present to the pupil; yet neither is it one that can be ignored.

An *Art History and Critical Studies* programme needs to establish the conditions in which the principle of pluralism in visual representation can be recognised and valued. This objective can be pursued by placing increased emphasis on those areas of cultural production traditionally regarded as marginal to European cultural history, thereby destabilising to some extent the dominant notion of the 'norm'. Where such cultural production is seen to be more than merely complementary to the European heritage, and similarly permeated with an equivalent sense of permanence and continuity, the value and significance of cultural diversity, with all its wider connotations, can be better approached and studied. In particular, some experience of the artistic products of non-European cultures, supported by an understanding of the need to enquire into the conditions of their original production, can help to establish an appreciation of the types of factors which might determine formal diversity. To the same end, the scope of study within western art history might be expanded to address the more neglected areas of pre-Renaissance art, where the preponderance of abstracted and distorted pictorial forms might be evaluated by the methods of contextualised study.

The aim cannot be to engage with the finer sophistications of signification diversely vested in the use of formal distortion either in this range of artistic production, or in twentieth century avant-garde art. The more fundamental aim must be to demonstrate the principle that technical skill and artistic value may be variously defined according to a diversity of social and cultural conditions, and in the process encourage a tolerance of less familiar formal modes. The practice must serve to identify the issues of skill, quality and value as problematic in artistic production, and consequently within art historical debate. A consideration of the function, status and character of artistic production in a variety of societies will raise such issues. Inevitably, an appreciation of the more specific use of these questionable values as signifiers within the art of this century can only develop from such informed attitudes.

It is important not to lose sight of the objective, which is to provide a critical framework enabling the pupil to proceed beyond a superficial knowledge of the visually given. It is aimed to provide the means towards the (open) end, not the end itself. Implicated in this process is the ability to identify the types of issues which it is necessary to address in the development of a fuller understanding; but this will involve a continuous and direct engagement with the objects of study. The skills and approaches are integral to the very discipline, and as such they develop in direct proximity to the specialist body of knowledge. They should not be characterised as a separate process, developed apart from the knowledge and subsequently applied to it. Conversely, the objects of study should not be put aside on the assumption that the skills relevant to their study will be developed elsewhere.

It is acknowledged that interdisciplinary skills make an increasing contribution to study as the pupil matures, but it is argued that there should be no circumstances in which the art history teacher temporarily abandons responsibilities to other disciplines because the going has got rough. Therefore, where intellectual structures are particularly complex, as in Brandon Taylor's example of modern culture, the material needs to be subjected to continuous reappraisal with a positive view to discovering possible points of access for the pupil. To conclude that these do not exist within the discipline itself is to negate the value of the discipline *per se*.

To arrive at such a conclusion would also be tantamount to a denial of majority access to the cultural heritage. This is especially ironical where the dispute focuses on the arena of twentieth century avant-garde art, wherein debates concerning intellectualism, lucidity and accessibility have been central issues in both theory and practice. Far from being resolved, these issues still maintain a high profile in much contemporary cultural practice, which the pupil-citizen will inevitably come to evaluate with or without the assistance of a foundation course in *Art History and Critical Studies*. Where it is considered that intellectualism in twentieth century art is the expression of a crisis in art practice, with wider connotations in social issues, then the value to be placed on a facility for informed and intelligent critical interpretation must be especially great.

Art commentary, it is often remarked, has become a twentieth century industry which has helped to create a minority specialist audience for art. Failure by educationists to address the area of modern cultural production will perpetuate the denial of access to the majority.

References

1 *Cf* Brandon Taylor's arguments in Chapter 9.
2 See DYSON, A. 1987. Style, Technique, Context: Art and Design History in the GCSE, *Journal of Art and Design Education*; Vol. 6, No. 2, pp. 149–58.
3 LONDON AND EAST ANGLIA GROUP FOR GCSE EXAMINATIONS. 1988. *Critical Studies in Art and Design (for Mature Candidates)*; syllabus for 1988.
4 CORK, R. 1976. *Vorticism and Abstract Art in the First Machine Age* Vol. 1 (London, Gordon Fraser) p. 225.

Chapter Eleven

ANTHONY DYSON Art History in Schools: a Comprehensive Strategy

This paper suggests a strategy for teaching the history of art in schools; and it had better begin with a defence of the term 'history of art'. To many teachers, and to their pupils, the term is intimidating and tends to conjure up the caricature of the art historian as inhibitor of creativity, and as virtually inimical to the warmly human pursuit of 'art appreciation' and the expression of personal views that this entails. The fact is that no proper art historian would ever have embarked on his profession *without* an enthusiastic appreciation of art, nor would he progress very far in it without the confidence to adopt a personal viewpoint and to propose new ways of attaining an understanding of the subject.

Whilst there seems to be a growing inclination among teachers of art to include in their courses a signficant element of appraisal, many oppose the notion of *history* of art, proposing 'appreciation', 'criticism', 'visual education', 'visual communication', 'cultural studies' and other terms to suggest something more liberal and unfettered by chronology. Yet art history nurtures an appreciation, not only of art objects but of visual experience in general; it depends upon the development of critical faculties; it effectively provides a visual education; it examines the way in which (or, perhaps, whether or not) art communicates; it provides a rich core to more wide-ranging cultural studies; and it can impart, possibly more vividly than any other aspect of history, a clear view of the perspective of time that is the setting for all human events and an understanding of which is the prerogative of all educated persons. History of art encompasses all this. Moreover concern with design, craft, film, photography, and the humblest as well as the most imposing objects and images is the business of a student of the subject.

In what follows an argument will be made for: (1) the need for structure in the teaching of the subject; (2) an acknowledgement that the traditional structures eminently suitable for pupils with certain aptitudes, and a certain degree of maturity, are less likely to meet the needs of others; (3) the devising of courses in primary schools and in the lower levels of secondary education, which will enrich the learning of all pupils, the majority of whom will never aspire to examination success in history of art; and (4) the use of such courses as a sensible preparation (of a kind which, in British schools at least, is at present virtually non-existent) for the relatively small number of pupils who *will* eventually take examinations in the subject.

A complex network of the ideas of prominent art historians and critics constitutes for us what may be called the sub-stratum of art history teaching. I propose the term 'sub-stratum' since ideas such as these find their way, sometimes unobtrusively and scarcely identified, into the consciousness (or sub-consciousness) of many of us, and are likely from their underground location to play an important part in determining pedagogical attitudes. A critical understanding by teachers of this ideological sub-stratum can help clarify the proliferation of questions that arises from it; the roots of such questions may more precisely be traced; and their relevance to the interests, knowledge and intellectual capacity of pupils may perhaps more accurately be gauged.

Above all, having recognised the structures we ourselves have adopted, albeit sometimes passively, in order to help us make sense of the welter of information and ideas that the study of art comprises, we are far more likely to be sensitive to the need for structure in our teaching. In *The Process of Education* (1960), Jerome Bruner is at pains to explain what he meant by defining education as the cultivation of excellence: helping each pupil, not only the most able, to achieve his optimum intellectual development. 'Good teaching' he insists

> that emphasises the structure of a subject is probably even more valuable for the less able . . . than for the gifted . . . for it is the former rather than the latter who (are) most easily thrown off the track by poor teaching [1].

The structure of a subject: what might this mean? Does the history of art 'have' a structure? Perhaps one of the most fundamental mistakes any student can make is to assume the existence in any subject of an underlying structure awaiting his conformity. The structure of the history of art is, no less than that of any other subject, a matter for proposal by individual scholars. Benedetto Croce, in his *Theory of Aesthetic* (1909), made the following scathing comment on 'historians who profess to wish to interrogate the facts without adding anything of their own'. 'This is at best the result of ingenuousness', he said, 'they will always add something of their own if they be truly historians' [2]. No historian—whether of art or of any other aspect of human activity— can *reproduce* the past. He can only recreate it. It is accepted by most philosophers of history that history is what historians write; and that

> no one but a mere collector of unrelated facts can put together the smallest narrative of human doings unless he have a determined point of view . . . a personal conviction of his own regarding the facts whose history he has undertaken to relate [3].

It is worth nothing in this context that the art historian or critic embarking on the arrangement of an exhibition, or the curator categorising his museum's permanent collection; or—and this is of course vitally important for our present purpose—the teacher of art displaying pupils' work, perhaps alongside the reproduced works of professional artists, have thereby the power to express personal convictions and interpretations and are thus responsible through the classifications and juxtapositions they adopt, for shaping the perceptions of viewers.

It goes without saying that the more extensive one's knowledge of a subject may be (and such knowledge may well be accumulated initially, at least, on the basis of structures proposed by others more expert) and the surer one's grasp of its complexities, the more likely will be one's ability to propose sensible, facilitating structures. But this in itself is an idea worth transmitting to pupils: the idea that any field of study is so virtually limitless that a process of simplification, of selection, is necessary in order to help us gain some kind of conceptual map of it; and that what scholars in any field are engaged in is a continual redrawing of the maps that propose the structures of their subjects.

A glance at most history of art examination syllabuses in this country will suggest to the prospective candidate that the subject has an immutable structure: that the history of art is necessarily ordered according to a succession of more or less clearly identifiable styles, conforming to particular stages in the development of man and therefore manifesting themselves during specific phases of history. Terms such as Classical, Byzantine, Carolingian, Mediaeval, Renaissance, Baroque, Rococo, Neo-Classical and Romantic; labels like Impressionism, Fauvism, Cubism, Futurism, Vorticism and Surrealism; the names of celebrated artists and the identification of key dates: these articulate the structure. Now, none of this is to be despised; far from it. It is a perfectly useful way of categorising and presenting the facts; but, with the needs of pupils in the lower age ranges (say, 9 to 13 or 14) in mind, I propose three basic objections—not to the existence of this familiar structure but to an uncritical and exclusive adoption of it. The first is that it is conducive to a certain kind of specialisation, a concentration within particular chronological and cultural limits; the second is that, generally, only the most prestigious works of art and architecture are accommodated by it; and thirdly, that it necessitates an approach that is either unsuitable or too difficult, or both, (and the distinction is deliberate) for all but what we might term 'academically inclined' pupils.

In the preface to his book *Rococo to Revolution* (1966) [4], Michael Levey, '. . . not wishing to be treated like a donkey', expressed the hope that he chose his subject for reasons other than that the eighteenth century was somehow his 'field'. The idea that an art historian must have a special 'field' (in spite of very many eminent exceptions) and that therefore the way for school pupils to master the subject is to concentrate (perhaps after a brief 'general survey') on a particular art-historical pasture has its origins in traditional university procedures inherited by and large from wholly admirable nineteenth century antecedents in German scholarship. GCE examinations in history of art are naturally structured so as to select and initiate those pupils most suited to benefiting from the kind of course offered in most universities; but this process of a downward permeation of influence from higher education is what determines the approach to most art history teaching (where it takes place) in general education. It is by no means certain that the model of the academic art historian is appropriate for the majority of the school population; in fact, it is highly unlikely.

There is, of course, much to be said for specialisation; but there has been a pronounced tendency in Britain—except perhaps at the primary level of education—to regard *generalisation* as somehow incompatible with serious scholarship. The affording of a general bird's-eye view of a subject is, it is frequently acknowledged, appropriate for young pupils, and perhaps even for undergraduates being introduced to a new study;

125

but, at least in the case of the latter, such general surveys are as often as not provided so that 'the serious business of concentration on a special area' may ultimately be engaged in.

The scaffolding of styles, movements, names and dates referred to above is not, of course, to be rejected. Much valuable teaching and learning has been—and will no doubt continue to be—facilitated by its bolstering; but neither is the obdurate bolting together of that scaffolding and its premature and exclusive adoption likely to lead to the more general inclusion in the secondary school curriculum of a subject which in its present form is studied by only a small minority of pupils, and studied by this small minority for only a very fleeting fragment of school life. History of art in British education may perhaps best be represented as the apex of a pyramid, floating baseless. It is considered that the subject may appropriately be studied in higher education (or as a direct preparation for procedure to that level) but that the systematic provision in primary and secondary school of what could, indeed should, be not merely a preface to specialist study but (even for pupils who may never aspire to examination success of any kind) a crux of the curriculum, is somehow unnecessary, or perhaps unsuitable. There is little doubt that what tends to restrict the appearance in schools of history of art is its very title, with the implied concentration on the great artistic manifestations of salient epochs in the history of mankind: an impression that, as we have suggested, is confirmed by the majority of examination syllabuses. One of our vital tasks as teachers is, as John Dewey in *Art as Experience* (1934) reminds us,

> to restore continuity between the refined and intensified forms of experience that are works of art, and everyday events, doings and sufferings that are universally recognised to constitute experience.
> Mountain peaks do not float unsupported . . . [5].

Even if they could, they would be unattainable. Making art accessible to the majority of school pupils will hardly be accomplished if the foothills of mundane experience are not shown to be relevant. It is hardly to be wondered at that the term 'history of art' is intimidating to many teachers and their pupils and that there now exists, almost by way of reaction, a nomenclature indicating the wish for a wide spectrum of approaches to visual experience: a spectrum extended to include considerably more of the visual world than fine art and architecture. Design education, environmental education, and film and television studies have all been influential in this broadening. All the opportunities seem now to exist for an educationally salutary linking of art history and associated disciplines; but if this is to be achieved, alternative structures for the subject need to be acknowledged.

Admitting the feasibility of alternative structures would make history of art more easily recognisable as a valuable meeting ground for a range of disciplines. The assumption that history of art is *above all* a study of style and iconography characterising the works of highly gifted individuals is unduly restrictive. If it could be accepted that history of art provides an equally legitimate opportunity for a study of the working methods of artists, architects, designers, craftsmen and collaborating

126

artisans, it would more easily be seen that pupils of various inclinations (whether 'arts' or 'sciences' based, to use the popular, crude generalisation) could find relevance and satisfaction in the field. A concept of history of art that embraces technical as well as stylistic and other considerations could provide an ideal curriculum 'junction box'. Earlier, the distinction was drawn between the *unsuitability* for some pupils and the *difficulty* for others of the traditional European approach to the study of history of art. It should at this point be emphasised again that one is by no means seeking to discredit such an approach. Those who argue that its abandonment would lead to nebulousness should certainly be heeded. The teaching of any subject should be based on a clear strategy, but if any given strategy presents more than salutary difficulty for some pupils, it seems reasonable to propose that alternative ways of rendering the content more accessible to them be found; and if unsuited to the interests and inclinations of others, that a different (but in its own way no less demanding) slant be given to the subject.

It would be too much of a digression if I were here to summarise the important work of the many educationalists who have drawn our attention to the need for teachers to take into account the psychological factors that seem to determine different aptitudes in different pupils. It will perhaps be sufficient to mention the work of Binet, who proposed four distinguishable *types* of perceiver of art objects: the type happy with pure description; the type that seizes on the expressive aspect; the type highly sensitive to mood; and the type with an inclination to acquire knowledge about the object [6]. It would obviously be naïve to assume that this categorisation is more than a convenient way of making the point that different human beings have what we might call different attitudes to seeing; that they 'feel' differently about what they see and, we may conclude, come to know and to understand by differing means. Art history, as traditionally taught, frequently has the now familiar charge of élitism levelled at it. This is to a large extent unfounded; but if what Binet would call the *type d'érudit*, the type with a facility for gathering and retaining knowledge, is alone catered for in art history syllabuses, credibility is lent to the accusation.

I propose now to turn to ways of making history of art a fundamental learning experience in general education—an experience that may profitably be offered to pupils from the primary level of schooling. Whilst fully acknowledging the importance of acquainting pupils with original artefacts, however prestigious or humble, what follows will be restricted to a discussion of what may be achieved in an ordinary classroom with the aid of a pile of postcard reproductions and photographs, a few colour transparencies, and a collection of everyday objects.

An acceptance of the principle that new learning may more effectively be founded upon what is already known suggests strategies whereby pupils may be guided (initially somewhat obliquely perhaps) in the direction of an understanding of the history of art. One such strategy may be based on a calculated and progressive series of comparisons of artefacts, images and visual experiences of all kinds: calculated and progressive, since particular comparisons are likely to raise particular questions the nature of which will have to be considered in relation to the needs, interests and degree of understanding of particular pupils or groups of pupils. For example, the contemplation of a group of Cubist portraits, however eloquently supported by a teacher's commentary, may mean little to pupils whose previous looking and questioning has left them unprepared for a difficult feat of perceptual gymnastics and probably unsympathetic towards images for which there may be no niche in their interest and experience. The way towards an appreciation of such images may need to be paved by a thorough consideration of their essential animating principles. In the case of the Cubist portraits, one such principle might be that of distortion; and it is suggested that, long before a Cubist portrait can be comprehended *as a Cubist portrait*, the formal principle of distortion (among other important characteristics) will need to be appraised, explored and understood by pupils. Such explorations will profitably include a consideration of examples within the scope of pupils' existing interests and experience—examples which need have no link with art beyond the fact that they happen to be illustrative of the particular principle or principles under consideration. The vital property of such examples will be their capacity to bridge pupils' existing awareness and their ultimate understanding of particular art objects.

Whatever the study of history of art may comprise, and however rigorous such study may eventually become for an individual pupil or student, it is as likely as in other areas of knowledge that he will need to be led systematically towards it. What has become in this country the traditional structure for art-historical studies is likely to make far more sense to the pupil ultimately needing to adopt it if it has been approached from the standpoint of early and frequent looking with no necessity to learn and remember names, dates and locations. What is important, though, is that a *sense* of human shaping, of chronology, of location, and of cultural inflection be gained, almost by contagion: a realisation that an art object is the work of human hand and mind, the evidence of a particular moment of history, the product of a certain geographical region and the expression of a culture. An awareness of the various intentions behind artefacts and the technical means by which they are given form; a consciousness of the fact that all things are not possible at all times or even in all places; and the discovery that art production is not the prerogative of Western civilisation: the work of provoking all these is something that should not be delayed in the education of any child. A pupil is much more likely to achieve a grasp of art history in the light of several years' opportunity to explore the world of visual imagery and develop, accept and respect the intuitive faculties which will render more vital the acquired items of knowledge. Insights into the motives and procedures of Western artists are more likely to be formed in the context of an awareness of those of artists of other cultures. Concentration on any particular historical period is likely to be imbued with more meaning if against the background of some knowledge, however general, of other times.

How could a course for primary school pupils and those in the early years of secondary schooling be structured, and how might it provide an appropriate modulation from the encouragement of general visual sensitivity to serious art-historical study? It would seem essential to base the approach on a system of comparisons.

The technique of comparison is widely used in art history teaching in higher education. Inviting students to seek similarities and differences in related images is an effective means of compelling them to look and to think. One polytechnic lecturer, John Walker (writing in Middlesex Polytechnic's journal *Block*, [7], has enlarged interestingly on the hazards and complexities of the system as well as its advantages. In presenting comparisons to children, however, at least two factors need to be kept in mind: first, that we can learn much from pupils' responses to what we show them, and would be well advised to heed these promptings in any selection we may make; and second, that sharply contrasting images are far likelier than closely similar ones to provide an effective starting point for younger pupils. The first consideration scarcely needs amplifying: a flexible attitude on the part of the teacher and the avoidance of stock comparisons (with the attendant risk of deadening experience and blunting perception), and involving pupils in discussion so that they may more readily develop a framework of language to assist understanding are clearly desirable. Any student of linguistics will confirm the importance of the second: to attempt to teach a person the meaning of the word 'brown' by presenting to him *only* brown objects (however many and in however many shades of the colour) will prove infinitely more frustrating for both teacher and pupil than by contrasting the brown with objects of other hue [8]. The brownness—and, incidentally, the blueness, yellowness, or redness of the objects juxtaposed with the brown—will thus become more easily graspable and the link between the word and the perceptual experience it signifies will be more surely forged. Brown is brown by virtue of all the other colours it is *not*; a Cubist painting is a Cubist painting by virtue of the fact that it is not an Impressionist or a Fauve or a Futurist or any other kind of painting. Furthermore, a Cubist painting by Picasso is recognisable as such by virtue of the fact that it is not a painting by Braque or any other Cubist—but this, of course, is where things get difficult!

It has been contended above that the structure of the history of art is a matter for proposal by individual scholars. Similarly, the shaping of the practically limitless volume of visual material that could feasibly be used in schools is a matter for initiation by individual teachers. A heavy reliance on 'packaged' material and a dependence on what have been referred to as 'teacher-proof curricula' are the very antithesis of the flexible approach most likely to stimulate the interest of pupils. Doing a little sorting exercise with a hundred (or more) postcard reproductions of paintings can be a valuable step in the direction of the structuring process. What might the possible criteria for classification be? What about the polarity complexity/simplicity? Having decided which is the most complex image and which the simplest (and if the exercise is undertaken by two or more persons there is sure to be considerable debate on the matter of selection) the business of arranging all the other images on a scale from complexity to simplicity could be tackled. Other polarities such as crudeness/refinement, verticality/horizontality, order/chaos, obscurity/definition, lightness/darkness, depth/flatness are further possibilities.

The foregoing is proposed simply by way of encouragement to teachers to proceed with confidence; and to emphasise that what is offered below is suggestion rather than prescription.

Consider the following categories of comparison:

1 *A comparison of reproductions of art objects with visual records of experiences familiar to pupils, or with every-day objects.*

An example of this kind of comparison might be a photograph of a greengrocer's stall set alongside one of a Byzantine mosaic.

This might give rise to such questions as:

In what ways are the images alike?

In what ways are they different?

Why should one be thought a work of art, the other not?

2 *A comparison of different art objects with similar subject matter (or different buildings erected for a similar purpose).*

Examples of this kind of comparison might be a reproduction (or a transparency, of course) of a Cubist head and a Renaissance portrait juxtaposed; or the Roman Colosseum set beside Wembley Stadium. In addition to the fundamental questions regarding difference and similarity, others are likely to be raised, including:

How were the respective items made?

By what kind of person or persons was each made?

For what kind of person or persons was each made?

For what purpose might each have been made?

3 *A comparison of pupils' own work in art with appropriate art objects.*

The whole matter of the integration of the production and the appraisal of art in schools deserves full and separate treatment. The opportunities offered by such links may be hinted at by the following questions:

How do I draw (or otherwise represent or express) the things I see (or imagine)?

How do I feel about the things I see (or imagine)?

Do my drawings look 'real'?

Do I intend them to look real?

How can I make them look more real?

Are there artists whose work mine resembles?

In what ways?

Are there ways of drawing other than mine?

How do different artists draw?

What makes them draw differently?

Do different artists *see* differently?

Do they *think* differently?

Is it this that makes them draw differently?

4   *A comparison of artefacts of different periods.*

Questions such as these might spring from this kind of comparison:

When might each item have been made?

Recently?

Long ago?

About how long ago?

What evidence that it is old or recently made does each contain?

How might a number of items be arranged chronologically?

What could such an arrangement tell us about changes in how people see or in what they like?

5   *A comparison of various products of a particular period: choice not restricted to art objects, nor even to visual material.*

Study based on comparisons of this kind could lead to a realisation of the essential 'untidiness' of history. If, for example, a coronation photograph of Edward VII and Alexandra were to be shown beside a Fauve painting produced at more or less the same moment in history; or if a poster advertising an early motor car were to be juxtaposed with a photograph of, say, Boccioni's sculpture 'Unique Forms of Continuity in Space' (1913), something of the avant-garde nature of the chosen art objects might more clearly be seen by pupils, and the bewilderment experienced by contemporaries could be sensed more deeply. A consideration of such material could give rise to questions such as:

When does each item look as if it was produced?

What evidence of date is to be found in the item itself; and what related evidence is available?

Do any items appear to be 'ahead of their time'?

Or 'behind the times'?

Is there such a thing as 'the spirit of an age'?

Would any particular object—or depiction—have been possible at any period other than the one in which it was produced?

Or in any other place?

6   *A comparison of art objects of a given School or period.*

This is the kind of task facing most prospective examination candidates, who will need to consider such questions as:

In what ways are the works similar?

In what ways are they different?

Are there stronger 'family resemblances' between the works of this period (or School, or culture) than between those of other periods?

Has the artist any importance as an individual during the period under review?

Assuming he can be identified as an individual, how does what we know about him influence the way we view his work?

How does the work of one artist seem to have influenced that of another?

In conclusion, the submission is that the close examination and analysis of particular works of art expected of serious students of the subject is hardly possible unless on the basis of a broad map of experience such as that proposed above. The family ambience supplies such experience for a fortunate minority; enterprising teachers have the task of providing it for the rest. Questions related to this kind of analysis are likely to be limitless in number and difficult even to formulate without much previous understanding of art and an adequate knowledge of the context in which the work under scrutiny was produced. In the history of art, the student is faced with a discipline to which there appears to be no easy and immediate access; a discipline the mastery of which involves the slow, deliberate acquisition of knowledge and insight by means similar to those hinted at here. It seems we should take seriously the exhortation of a London teacher [9]: that we should devise ways not only of making history of art a feasibility in the early years of schooling, but that we should do everything possible to bring about an effective modulation between what happens in the teaching and learning of the subject at that level and what is already well established at higher levels of education. This paper has proposed an approach; failure to achieve a sensible link-up is likely only to result in more of the fragmentation we find it so difficult to avoid in art education in general.

Notes and References

1 BRUNER, J. 1960. *The Process of Education*. Harvard; p. 9.
2 CROCE, B. 1909. *Theory of Aesthetic*. Nonpareil, 1978; pp. 133–5.
3 *Ibid*.
4 LEVEY, M. 1966. *Rococo to Revolution*. London, Thames and Hudson.
5 DEWEY, J. 1934. *Art as Experience*. New York, Paragon; p. 3.
6 For a brief summary see READ, H. 1943. *Education through Art*. London, Faber, 1970; p. 93.
7 WALKER, J. 1980. *Block* No. 1. Middlesex Polytechnic.
8 For an interesting discussion of Saussure and semiology see CULLER, J. 1976. *Saussure*. London, Fontana.
9 GOODWIN, B. of Godolphin and Latymer School, during a meeting organised by the ILEA Art Inspectorate at the London College of Printing. 16 Sept. 1981.

Chapter Twelve

TONY COLLINS Before the Vanishing Point: Some Perspectives on Teaching Art History to Studio Practitioners

Everything begins and ends with the need to understand history; that is, the present Hadjinicolaou [1].

The compulsory study of art history in schools and colleges of art followed the introduction of the Diploma in Art and Design more than two decades ago. For several difficult and troubled years, those who were charged with the task of teaching art history at diploma and pre-diploma levels strove manfully to win for their subject academic status and professional dignity commensurate with the prestige art history had enjoyed in the universities . . . in Germany at least . . . for over a century. Yet as the Summerson Committee discovered and as the student demonstrations of the late-sixties proved, they incurred only discontent and, on occasions, overt hostility. The art education establishment capitulated: in 'reviewing' the position of art history as an obligatory 'core' discipline, the *Joint Report of the NACAE and the NCDAD* entitled 'The Structure of Art and Design Education in the FE Sector', published in 1970, gave tacit consent and covert impetus to a devaluation of the subject in schools of art and design. As a result, many staff and sometimes whole sections were absorbed into the ubiquitous principalities of complementary and liberal studies.

In an article published in the *Times Educational Supplement* in 1979, Mary Acton approved the fact that through the framework of the CNAA the history of art could now be made more 'flexible'—a typically discreet euphemism for 'vulnerable' or 'pregnable'. Today, in many art and design courses validated by BTEC or the CNAA, a renewed emphasis upon a narrow, market-led, vocational training is furthering the erosion of art history initiated by the *Joint Report* . . . so much so that in some schools of art and design the history of art as an identifiable component of the curriculum has all but disappeared. Meanwhile, in response to the self-styled 'crisis' of art history, publications like *Block*, *Aspects* and *Artery*, as well as professional journals such as *J.A.D.E*, have made space available to academics and their perspectives—methodological and ideological—on the subject. However, 'perspectives' on the teaching of art history to studio practitioners are of little practical use or consequence if all we find at the end of our cone of vision is a blank screen and a lesson in curricular accountability. Sooner or later we must confront the more urgent and belligerent question of survival: should we allow art history to vanish from the curriculum of practical art and design courses, or can we establish the existence of authentic educational needs which

133

the study of art in history may best satisfy? Hence the rhetoric of the title to this paper: *before* the vanishing point.

Certainly if art history as an academic discipline remains wedded to orthodoxies which, derived from the writings of Dvorak, Burkhardt and Taine, conceive art *as* historical documentation, then the subject will have little to offer the school of art and design within the present ideological arena. Yet it is surprising to find, when one examines just what *is* practised under the rubric of art history, how many teachers continue to live on in the shadows of their Teutonic ancestors who decreed that the history of art could only aspire to academic status as a sub-discipline of the larger intellectual field of general HISTORY, and therefore confront the work of art as a form of historical documentation.

Now whatever claims are made for their subject by historians like Popper and Meyerhoff, history is primarily concerned with the reconstruction of past events, causations and chronologies. The historian's principal undertaking is to test the available data for accuracy and authenticity. He/she is not concerned with the material constitution or phenomenological status of that data beyond its function as 'evidence'. In short, the historian attempts to answer the question 'what happened?' . . . and as Feldman has remarked:

> aside from getting the record straight, this concern is unguided by
> an assumption that 'what happened' will happen again [2].

However, if history is built upon a framework of data *about*, not an experience *of*, events, then works of art are capable of surviving *as* events. They are not signals from the past through which events may be reconstructed, but primary structures which signal their coextensive presence within an existential present. Clearly, art history differs from general history in that access to knowledge is not sought through existing discourses upon events; rather, the object of study and the proposed object of knowledge is perceived as an event or discourse in its own right. For whereas the general historian undertakes to reconstruct an event from the past through an analysis of its *adherent signals*—that is, the discourses of evidence and documentation—the art historian undertakes to elucidate or explain an event from the primary datum of the event itself and the *self-signals* it issues. The very fact that works of art are capable of persisting through time as self-signalling events dismantles the commentaries of conventional histories of art—idealist or positivist—with their elaborate categories of adherent signals. If we expect our students of art and design to experience works of art as primary structures, as 'events in themselves', then it seems to me that a systematic or epistemic conceptualisation of a discrete curriculum field called 'art history' is untenable. And really there is not much point in pretending that it would amount to very much even if it *were* conceptually sound. For example, I have calculated that a student on a three year practical arts programme will spend, on average, a total of 162 hours or twenty-four working days in the art history department . . . should one be available to him or her! Hardly time enough to distinguish between Millais and Millet, let alone Wölfflin and Wollheim, *Geistesgeschichte und Geisteswissenschaft.*

In fact, the aims and methods of the historian of art have little in common with those of orthodox, specialist historians of politics, constitutions, societies or whatever, beyond a shared nomenclature. The orthodox historian undertakes to reconstruct past events through an examination of *post-festum* data. The art historian attempts to elucidate events from the primary datum of the event ART. Of course, the academic researcher will interest him/herself in problems of attribution, collaboration, classification and so on. Naturally the teacher of art history will try to make the fruits of academic research available to students. However, it should be obvious that the further we retreat into the past, the more fragmented or inaccessible our primary data are likely to become. It is illogical to suppose that we can transcend a lack of primary data by 'empathy' or 'intuition' since both court historical distortion; the illusions of the empathiser. All historical explanation which does not address itself to primary data is fictive and potentially fictitious. The history of art is riddled with lacunae and their fictitious reconstructions. For this reason I would agree with Pat Sloan that

> in a number of ways it is easier to study the present than the past
> since a greater amount of data is available, making it easier to
> separate the facts from the fictions [3].

More soberly, Harold Rosenberg has argued with great force that

> an enormous volume of significant information about works of art
> and their mode of generation has been accumulated in this century,
> and the failure to open this to the student deprives him of the only
> currently available equivalent to the atelier [4].

Sloan's emphasis upon the study of contemporary practices and Rosenberg's notion of art history as an essential information bank are in themselves justifications for including the history of art as a component of practical arts curricula. If we allow historical perspectives upon current practices to vanish from the curriculum, then we are indeed guilty of perpetuating an act of deprivation, sensory and intellectual. However, beyond the rather vague recommendation that

> perhaps there ought to be more leeway for planning individual
> projects which combine art historical study with related studio
> experience . . . [5],

neither Sloan nor Rosenberg pursue this line of argument, as a methodological proposition for teaching art history in the school of art and design, to its logical conclusions. For if we choose to abandon the traditions of academic address in favour of a synchronic examination of *primary* data and *significant* information, then surely we should begin by structuring art history syllabi around the 'atelier' itself . . . that is, the current studio practices of our own students.

There are, I suggest, three good reasons for adopting this approach:
1   In the first instance, a syllabus constructed upon a framework of first-hand experiences locates the student, his/her needs, predispositions and goals—not the subject teacher, nor the taught subject—at the very centre of our pedagogical rationale. The problems of syllabus design or subject content cannot therefore be reduced to solutions which propose orthodox, apriori categories of stylistics or thematics, nor to a monolithic

theory of art *as* history. For that syllabus will be governed by the specificities and dynamics of studio practice itself. Osborne has established how much easier it is to learn rationally that which we already sense intuitively, and has described how it is the 'unreflective performance which can be relied upon to come into operation' without excessive effort, from 'inside' the individual, which leads to that necessary 'tautening of attention, concentration of control, heightening and enhancement of consciousness'—without which 'understanding' cannot be underwritten [6]. In other words, new learning is most effective when founded upon existing knowledge or experience. It is this state of effortless concentration which all teachers of all subjects strive to induce in their students, and which the teacher of art history may more realistically promote through a teaching programme founded upon the direct experiences of studio practice.

2   This approach would also help counter the familiar accusation that art historians ignore 'contemporary ideas and movements in art' and that art history 'lacks any connection with work in the studio' [7]. In my experience, most students of art and design are not endemically resistant to the disciplines of theoretical analysis and historical exegisis; only to that genre of academic commentary which assiduously avoids all reference to the contemporary world. Any model of art history which seeks to *justify* the past will hold little interest for those who are immersed in the present. Instead, I am proposing a model for reorientation which embraces both the existential present of making art and the co-existent presence of works from the past as the route and roots of contemporary practice.

3   Finally, the model of art history proposed here is fundamentally *critical* in spirit. Although it positions studio practice at the very centre of the pedagogical rationale, it will not necessarily give support to those who 'resent old fashioned'—that is, historically informed—'explanations of what is uniquely new' [8]. As Mary Acton has remarked, in far too many schools of art and design, demonstrably

> immature students are not expected to allow their work to develop
> from experience nor to study traditional methods in any depth, but
> are required to become immediately members of the avant-garde [9].

Yet the very idea of an 'avant-garde' reproduces *outmoded*, positivistic ideologies like Winckelmann's doctrine of 'inevitable progress' or Riegl's 'divine plan' whereby the cult of the individual personality or 'artist as genius' becomes an impeditive notion in the *service* of a dominant ideology and cultural hegemony . . . and leads only to mystification and non-intervention.

However, it is a central premise of my argument that a history of art for studio practitioners should be both elucidatory and interventionist. By shifting the pedagogical focus away from traditional considerations of 'biography' and 'personality' towards a thorough analysis of material production and process, art history may intervene between a reductive historicism on the one hand, and an institutionalised avant-gardism on the other. At the very least, a materialist history of art will challenge the orthodox notion that what is 'new' is of necessity 'unique'. Of course, in fine art departments where the study of drawing is even now still regarded as a 'reactionary' enterprise, or in departments of visual communications where the principles of colour perception are exclusively a matter for 'market research' not aesthetic discrimination, then art history may well appear to be an anachronism. However, I contend that it is within such contexts that the loss of the art historian would indeed amount to a state of pedagogical deprivation.

It is possible that any proposed reorientation of art history away from orthodox models of *Geistesgeschichte und Geisteswissenschaft* towards an alloyage of theory and practice, history and criticism, will appear to follow the strategem outlined by Irving Sandler in his essay entitled *New Ways of Teaching Art History*, whereby current studio activities are used as a platform for hypothesising about the art of the past [10]. In fact, I am opposed to Sandler's notion of using 'current perspectives as access to the past', simply because it returns us to the methodological impasse of a *post-festum*, historical *justification*. Art history is slipped in through the studio back door disguised as a surrogate artist's model, complete with pendulous breasts and varicose veins; a studio 'prop', like the worm-holed donkeys and filthy sinks—a traditional talisman of institutionalised art education. We are invited to glance in her direction and, barely containing our disgust, remark how *our* ideal of the human female form (slim, sleek and sun-tanned) has changed since . . . whenever.

On the contrary, I proposed that the art historian invokes the *past* as access to the *present*, in order to inform, elucidate and, when necessary, intervene by requisitioning studio activities. Such interventions will demonstrate that much contemporary art practice is meaningless *except* in terms of the past, immediate and distant. For whereas the general historian attempts to describe past events without assuming that 'what happened' will happen again, the art historian operating within the conceptual framework outlined here will attempt to elucidate and inform what is happening now *because* it happened in the past and will continue to happen in the foreseeable future.

The idea of 'reorientation' implies a specific curricular initiative and attendant syllabus proposals, which I shall proceed to delineate below. However, at this stage of the argument it may prove useful to review the steps advanced in this paper so far. Whereas the general historian attempts to reconstruct past events from the sum total of available data, the 'event' ART is itself the primary datum of art history. The codifications of such data—that is, the specific language-structures or systems of representation involved—are present to some degree and in some particular combination in all works of art, for that is what works of art *are*: coded visual representations mediated and materialised through modes of production. Such data can be explained 'as the data of any inspiration can be' [11]. From this perspective, the history of art may be construed as a history of mediations and materialisations, of modes of practice and production; in short, a history of art as the history of *recurring artistic problems*.

However, the external conditions which make it more possible to confront certain problems at certain times—and not others—and through which certain problems assume priority whilst others become marginalised, constitute a theoretical paradigm or tangential problematic. For example, the problem of perceptual or 'local' colour is tangential to the problematic 'realism' and the reflection theories of nineteenth century epistemologies; the problem of conceptual, symbolic or 'arbitrary' colour is tangential to the problematic 'expressionism' and the epistemological paradigm of pre-war German psychologism [12]. When problems cease to command active attention, the historical sequence of solutions is stabilised, and the codes and conventions of practice assume common currency. Yet, as Kubler has remarked, all problems are subject to reactivation under changed or new conditions [13]. Such conditions are not 'given', nor fixed for all time. Indeed, one lesson of the post-Modernist enterprise is that disparate problems may be reactivated or disregarded by a positive act (or negative failure) of will. From this perspective, art history is conceived as a history of theoretical paradigms or *recycled problematics*.

Underpinning this model of art history is a conceptualisation of art as a convention-governed practice or mode of production which resists orthodox 'hermeneutic' theories of interpretation. Before I proceed to discuss the role of the art historian working within this conceptual framework, it is necessary to examine the conceptual model itself in a little more detail.

Art history as the history of recurring artistic problems

The work of the French social anthropologist, Claude Lévi-Strauss, provides important cues for a proposed reorientation away from biographical or chronological modes of art historical address towards a material-structural analysis which, I contend, should determine modes of historical inquiry promoted in schools of art and design. His ethnographic analyses purport to uncover the basic and universal structural elements of mentalities, and point towards the existence of deep structures which 'lie beyond the empirical diversities of human societies' [14]. He describes how 'the fundamental structures of the mind are the same everywhere and do not undergo any structural development', so that

> between one period and another in history or between one society
> and another, it is not the cognitive structures of the mind which
> differ, but the problems which men raise for themselves [15].

So, although 'new' minds may discover new meanings in a work of art (that is, the 'interpretation of content mode'), the structural problem of giving form to content remains a cognitive constant. Because the 'problem of form mode' refers to those isomorphic structural elements which do not vary from mind to mind, from generation to generation, or from epoch to epoch, the very idea of 'progress' in art is based upon false premises.

From the related field of synchronic linguistics we discover that such structural elements evolve, dissolve and reappear throughout history,

138

irrespective of the 'meaning' or 'content' which they carry so that

> phoneme A, occurring in an earlier stage of a language becomes
> phoneme B at a later stage, independent of meaning and only under
> the rules governing the phonetic structure of language [16].

Kubler concludes that these syntactic structures govern the formal infrastructure of every art, and therefore 'everything made now is either a replica or variant of something made some time ago and so on back' [17].

Now the problem with epistemological prescriptions of this kind, as with structuralist theory in general, issues from the idealist or anti-historical, anti-materialist undertones which they sustain. However, in the post-structuralist writings of Bourdieu we find a rationale for re-situating art practice as a problem-solving activity both within a field of *knowledge* and within *history*:

> Educated people of a given period may disagree on the questions
> they discuss but are at any rate in agreement about discussing
> certain questions . . .
>
> A thinker is linked to his period, and identified in space and time,
> primarily by the conditioning background of problem approach in
> which and by which he thinks [18].

In other words, works of art may be analysed by exploring the dialectical interplay between problem/practice—question/solution, which in turn occupies a dialectical relationship with that particular frame of problematic reasoning which defines the epistemological map of a given period or society. So we arrive at a theoretical justification for the history of art as the history of recurring artistic problems.

On a more practical level it is now possible to see how we might approach existing works of art from the perspective of the *practitioner*, the *student* of visual problems. For, within this conceptual framework, all works of art propose solutions—coherent or fragmented, original or replicate, willed or fortuitous, successful or unsuccessful—to problems of material representation and realisation. Each work of art represents one among many possible solutions to a particular problem surfacing from a frame of problematic reasoning. Because we can only come to terms with events through their linguistic identities, it is the very 'chain' of solutions which continuously defines and redefines the problem. We may term each chain of like solutions a form-class. Art history as a history of recurring artistic problems circumnavigates the teleological quicksands of conventional histories of art; for the chain of solutions which composes the form-class held by a frame of problematic reasoning cuts cleanly across orthodox classifications of style (formalism) or theme (iconography). Nor does it reproduce élitist distinctions between master-piece and minorpiece, high art and popular art, fine art and the applied arts or even between 'art' and 'design'. The very concept of a form-class widens the historical frame of reference to embrace *all* visual artefacts of an aesthetic order. Useful artefacts or functional objects consolidate or modify our environment; works of art consolidate or modify our perception of that environment. At this most practical of levels, the history of art merely coincides with the history of all man-made things.

Art history as a history of recurring artistic problems opposes 'les histoires evenementielle et conjoncturelle' of conventional histories of art with 'une histoire structural structurale', which is vertical, contrapuntal, serial . . . not necessarily sequential [19]. From this perspective we may explore the extent to which a Chinese scroll painting of the eleventh century occupies the same form-class—related to problems of perceptual 'closure'—as a late Jackson Pollock. We can explain how a Spanish Romanesque wall painting proposes one solution to the problem of split complementaries and spectral remainders as the 'Trellis' wallpaper of William Morris proposes another, and Monet's *Impression: Sunrise* proposes still another. We may reveal how Saenredam's attempt to solve the problem of multiple cones of vision in *The Grote Kerk at Haarlem* resurfaces centuries later in Van Gogh's *Bedroom at Arles* and later still in Braque's *Atelier* series. We may disclose how a Vallin interior at Nancy occupies the same form-class—unity/consistency of micro/macro structures—as St Peters in Rome and Nervi's Exhibition Hall in Turin.

Even the orthodox dynamics of conventional histories of art with their linear trajectories, 'necessary sequences' and patterns of 'inevitable progress' are outpaced and outdistanced by the concept of form-classes. But we can go further still: because each chain of solutions is demonstrably stretched across the 'given' or established landmarks of art history, we

43 PIETER SAENREDAM *The Grote Kerk at Haarlem*, 1636, oil on panel 23·5 × 32·25"; National Gallery, London.

44 VINCENT VAN GOGH
Bedroom at Arles, 1888, oil
on canvas 28·5 × 36″;
National Gallery, London.
(photo: Bridgeman
Art Library)

may safely assume that other solutions—new or replicate—will follow. It is therefore logical for the art historian to embrace the work of his/her own students within the same field of inquiry. The teacher who is alert to those problems currently preoccupying students in the studio, will seize upon them as a way of elucidating an existing chain of 'events' and of helping to shape its future direction. In this way, art history will offer the art student a framework against which he/she can measure personal practice. In this way art history may come alive.

In fact, the art historian may be in a *better* position that his/her studio-based colleagues to demonstrate—by exploring the historical determinants of space representation systems for example, or by unravelling the historical dialectics of perceptual and conceptual colour modes—how a visual improvisation of formal innovation becomes institutionalised as a canon for practice. He/she may then proceed to examine the various strategies artists in the past have used to subvert the prevailing conventions; and in the process perhaps explain how orthodox, stylistic labels like Mannerism or Romanticism or Cubism have become art historical mystifications which *prevent* us from 'seeing' the material struggles which artists associated with each 'ism' readily undertook against

141

the conditioning conventions of the period—risking personal and professional obscurity for a gain in formal vigour.

Finally, the art historian working within this conceptual framework is in the very best position to demonstrate that all works of art worthy of some attention, including the work of his/her own students, issue from a conflict between convention and invention, between recent and long established traditions. For we cannot evade the fact that inspiration and innovation are tied to frames of problematic reasoning laid down by the past, redefined by the present. A history of art which confronts the complexities of definition and redefinition, which integrates past and present, production and consumption, theory and practice . . . may encourage the student to view the subject not as some kind of enforced communion with the dead, but as a signal to the future and his/her place within it.

Art history as the history of recycled problematics

Wölfflin's dictum that 'not everything is possible at all times' refers to the general historical/theoretical context which surrounds any solution to a pictorial problem. Indeed, it invokes the epistemological paradigm of the problem itself. To the extent that no problem can be isolated from its historical, theoretical and epistemological framework, that framework constitutes a *problematic* [20]. In the field of art 'events', as soon as a solution to a particular problem is advanced, it may provide a model for subsequent solutions within the same problematic. In time, problems themselves become inert and will merely serve to consolidate the chain of solutions which constitute a form-class. So from one perspective the Norwood canvases of Pissarro or the Hampton Court paintings of Sisley consolidate proposals for solving the problem of local colour in changing natural light first advanced by the painters of the Barbizon School. Similarly, many textile designs by Arthur Silver and Christopher Dresser consolidate Morris's solutions to the problem of linear stylisation from organic sources. The complex spatial constructions of Piero della Francesca consolidate solutions to the problems of representing the three-dimensional world on a two-dimensional surface through the application of measured optical rule systems and empirical framing devices, first advanced by Giotto a century before.

However, the 'historical process' is not nearly as deterministic as it is often made to appear in conventional, historicist theories of art. Two artists could well be engaged in solving quite different problems whilst appearing to share the same structural problematic; or they may interpret the same problem in markedly distinctive ways. The problem of local colour for the generation of 1870 represents only one point of possible entry into the wider problematic of Realism. The problems of surface rhythms and organic stylisations which preoccupied Morris, Silver and Dresser are merely those which in a particular epoch and location issued from an underlying problematic which we can trace back to the Ancient Greeks and beyond . . . the problematic of Organic Abstraction. And of course, the problems of empirical measured perspective which both

45 GIOTTO *Life of Christ: Lamentation over the Body of Christ*, 1304–5, fresco in the Scrovegni Chapel, Padua. (photo: Mansell Collection)

46 PIERO DELLA FRANCESCA *The Baptism of Christ*, 1440–5, oil on panel 65·5 × 45·5"; National Gallery, London. (photo: Bridgeman Art Library)

Giotto and Piero addressed from very particular, personal 'viewpoints' are inseparable from the material problematic of visual representation and 'spectator space'.

Perhaps, as Georges Braque once remarked, 'progress in art does not consist in extending frontiers, but in knowing them better' [21]. Now clearly Braque did not intend his remark to be interpreted as a reductive axiom. For the artist always has a range of open possibilities. The selection of one particular solution in preference to another, as with one's choice of engagement from the range of problematics acutely evident at a specific historical conjuncture, cannot be explained away by orthodox notions of time or temper, chronology or progress, biography or ideology. To attempt to explain the origination and exploitations of a visual problematic is an eminently historical task, but a very delicate one. For the evidence exists primarily in the work of art itself. Therefore, any scheme to establish a history of art for studio practitioners must be conceived not as a theoretical assignment, but as a profoundly practical disquisition.

143

Inevitably, the history of art as a history of recycled problematics challenges the diachronic orthodoxies of conventional art history. On the way, many entrenched beliefs concerning form and content, style and theme, will be reappraised. I have already touched upon issues related to Realism and Abstraction. Other issues, which might form the constituent topics of an art history syllabus for studio practitioners, include Figuration, Narrative, Symbolism, Functionalism, Modernism and Avant-Gardism. In each instance, as soon as we abandon the constraints of chronology to focus upon the particular form-class constituted by a range of like solutions to problems surfacing from an identified problematic, we are encouraged to examine current approaches to the same theoretical paradigm. For example, the concept *realism* usually refers to an art historical term which describes a movement in art history *circa* 1850, associated with the work of Courbet, Millet and Daumier. The problematic *realism* refers to a range of visual problems which have been 'solved' by artists as different in time and temper as Caravaggio and Hopper, Ostade and Chuck Close. Outside the reified discourses of academic art history there is 'no one thing called realism but many *realisms* with different conditions of existence which secure their definite forms' [22]. As a visual problematic, 'realism' has been 'recycled' in major art exhibitions in this country on at least one half dozen occasions in the past eighteen months. It continues to be 'recycled' week by week in every school of art and design throughout the country.

In other words, I am suggesting that the alert art historian should choose to explore such problematics, which form the objects of current studio practice and debate, in order to inform and elucidate contemporary concerns through the provision of historical perspectives. In this way, the history of art will encourage the student to see him/herself as 'living history', in both senses of the phrase, that is, as both product of and catalyst upon 'events'. For the next link in the chain may well depend on the problems and problematics that he/she chooses to confront today . . . and tomorrow.

In place of strife: the art historian in the school of art and design

When art history first began to establish itself in Germany as an academic discipline, its tutelage of university professors and *Privatdozent* consisted very largely of scholars seconded from other more legitimate intellectual fields: archaeology, history, theology, philosophy, literature, and in one notable instance (Panovsky) law. The ensuing, protracted struggle for self identity and academic status within an acknowledged community of humanist scholars left its mark: an obsessive concern with 'objectivity' and 'science'. It followed that art historians of the English-speaking nations, weighed down by the imposing apparatus of Teutonic scholarship, were very careful to dissociate themselves from practical arts programmes which focused upon material production and processes. Even when Panovsky arrived in the USA in 1931 to teach graduate

144

students of art history, he unashamedly confesses how 'the new discipline had to fight its way out of of an entanglement with practical art instruction' [23]. At the same time, the 'humanist discipline' of art history was attempting to establish itself as a 'science' at the very point when the dynamics of Modernism had reached a level of visual and theoretical complexity which resisted nineteenth century systems of stylistic classification and thematic categorisation. So the professional art historian began to turn away from contemporary concerns, in order to immerse himself in the more unassailable but limiting problems of the past, and their historical reconstruction.

Naturally, when the professional art historian attempted to transplant the methodologies of academic research into the school of art and design, he/she found an audience of studio practitioners impatient with such reified discourses. Yet it was the art education establishment itself which countenanced this approach: the *First Coldstream Report* argued that

> the teaching of art history will need teachers qualified in the subject. First rate teachers are rare but we believe that the demand will increase the growth of the subject in the universities. The introduction of courses in the art schools . . . will indeed create a new demand and thus promote supply [24].

In fact, these words only *encouraged* the influx of university-based models for the teaching of art history into the arena of practical visual arts education. However, in the space of four years the art establishment was forced to think again. The Summerson Committee confessed that

> it is not necessarily the art historian with the highest academic qualifications who is the best teacher of art history in the college of art [25].

In reviewing the Summerson proposals, Quentin Bell conceded that the professional art historian, for whom the university or museum would provide a natural habitat, may well view the art school as 'alien territory' [26]. More recently Anthony Dyson suggested that the model of the academic art historian is 'perhaps inappropriate' for the majority of students who study the subject of art history as one component of a practical art course [27].

The historiography of art history discloses a very different story. In a paper entitled *The History of Art as a Humanistic Discipline*, Erwin Panovsky first drew up the demarcation lines between art theory, art history and art criticism which have since become commonplace. Only fifteen years ago Kleinbauer attempted to sharpen the distinctions between scholarship which is 'dispassionate' (that is, art history) and scholarship which is necessarily 'partisan' (that is, art criticism) [28]. Two years later we find Hadjinicolaou insisting upon the differences between

> art criticism which is concerned with contemporary art and which is therefore relevant to living artists, and art history, whose principal function is to explain past phenomena [29] . . .

as if the past were no longer 'relevant to living artists'!

However, it is my contention that the notion of professional autonomy for art historians—whether tenured to a university, saleroom or merchant bank—is pure mystification. For whenever that art historian confronts the primary datum of the event ART, past *or* present, his/her field of inquiry must lead to *critical* insights—that is, the domain of apparent passion and partisanship. Artificial distinctions between past and present practices, like the attempt to separate dispassionate 'fact' from paritisan 'feeling', unnecessarily limits our frames of reference. It is therefore futile to draw up distinctions between art history and art criticism, between past and present. They share the same epistemological map; they engage and occupy the same frames of problematic reasoning; they even apply the same investigative procedures to the same artistic problems. Criticism only lacks that which history feeds off: the warranty of adherent signals, the dead weight of 'treatise and theses' [30].

Yet, paradoxically, this is an analogous position to the situation in which teachers of practical arts disciplines find themselves as a matter of course, and in my experience they do not appear to feel unduly insecure before their students. I believe that the art historian should *confront* the open, untested spaces of the studio; that he/she should function first and foremost as 'scholar-critic in residence' [31]. It may be that the 'professional' art historian is not the best man or woman for the job. Pat Sloan has argued that art history in the school of art and design ought to be taught by artists [32]. Although I would hesitate to propose prescriptive measures upon this matter, it must be obvious that collaboration between art historians and studio practitioners will not come about until the art historian escapes from orthodox notions concerning the separation of theory and practice, production and consumption, history and criticism, past and present. Only then will he/she be ready to give critical support to the material experiences of studio practice.

Louis Pasteur once observed that fortune favours the prepared mind. It is the *unprepared* art historian who still regards contemporary art as a terrifying and senseless adventure; who provokes impatience with the study of art history from students of art and design; and who will be ultimately responsible for the disappearance of the subject from the curriculum . . . its eventual vanishing point. Yet the art historian could begin to prepare simply by spending more time in the studio. There he/she will soon discover that few misunderstandings exceed those between practitioners engaged upon solving very different kinds of visual problems. The art historian would then be in the very best position to elucidate those differences by unravelling the underlying problematics at issue. In this pursuit historical perspectives are visual ammunition; the target should be the material practices of art production *today*.

For too long art historians operating in schools of art and design have treated their students as adversaries, or have attempted to ensnare them in a net of adherent signals and orthodox, *post-festum* mystification. Yet surely Acton was right to suggest that

> the practical side of life has much to offer the academic and *vice
> versa*, if only each side could treat the other as equal rather than

rival. This is especially true in fields like art and art history where there should be so much common ground to start with [33].

Of course one must accept that the production and consumption of art are *not* identical social or institutional practices. However, as I have argued throughout this paper, neither are they pedagogically discrete. Only when the art historian becomes willing to lay aside the tools of academic corroboration for those of practical collaboration, will he/she be valued by studio practitioners for having para-sight; not anathematised as a parasite.

Notes and References

1 HADJINICOLAOU, N. 1973. *Art History and Class Struggle*. Pluto Press; p. 4.
2 FELDMAN, E. 1970. Engaging Art in Dialogue; in PAPPAS, G. (ed). *Concepts in Art and Education*. London, Macmillan; p. 358.
3 SLOAN, P. 1973. Teaching Art History in the Community College; in: BATT-COCK, G (ed). *New Ideas in Art Education*. Dutton; p. 115.
4 ROSENBERG, H. 1973. Educating Artists; in: BATTCOCK, *ibid*. Note 3; p. 101.
5 SLOAN, *ibid*. Note 3; p. 116.
6 OSBORNE, H. 1970. *The Art of Appreciation*. Oxford U.P.; p. 5.
7 MADGE, C. and B. WEINBERGER. 1973. *Art Students Observed*. London, Faber; p. 276.
8 FELDMAN, *ibid*. Note 2; p. 358.
9 ACTON, M. 1979. Does Art really need History? *Times Educational Supplement* Vol 389, 4 April 1980.
10 SANDLER, I. 1973. New Ways of Teaching Art History, in: BATTCOCK, *ibid*. Note 3; pp. 117–27.
11 ROSENBERG, *ibid*. Note 3; p. 101.
12 HAFTMANN, W. 1974. *Painting in the C20th; Vol. 2*. London, Lund Humphries; pp. 18–21.
13 KUBLER, G. 1962. *The Shape of Time*. Yale U.P.; p. 35.
14 LÉVI-STRAUSS, C. 1975. in: BOTTOMORE T. *Marxist Sociology*. London, Macmillan; p. 71.
15 LÉVI-STRAUSS, C. 1976. Personal Communication to the Author, in: GABLIK, S. *Progress in Art*. London, Thames and Hudson; pp. 33–38.
16 KUBLER; *Ibid*. Note 13; p. 123.
17 *Ibid*.
18 BOURDIEU, P. 1971. Systems of Education and Systems of Thought, in: YOUNG, M (ed) *Knowledge and Control: New Directions for the Sociology of Education*. London, Collier-Macmillan; p. 191.
19 BRAUDEL, F. 1981. in: ARMES, R. (ed) *Problems of Film History*. Middlesex Polytechnic Curriculum Centre for the History of Art and Design; p. 20.
20 See ALTHUSSER, L. 1969. *For Marx*. trans. BREWSTER. London, Allen Lane.
21 BRAQUE, G. 1969. *The Diaries 1917–1952*. in: MASINI, L. *Braque*. Hamlyn; p. 42.
22 WOLFF, J. 1981. *The Social Production of Art*. London, Macmillan; p. 93. My italics.
23 PANOVSKY, E. 1955. *Meaning in the Visual Arts*. Anchor; p. 324.
24 ASHWIN, C. 1975. *Art Education: Documents and Policies 1768–1975*. Society for Research into Higher Education; p. 99.
25 *Ibid*. p. 112.
26 BELL, Q. 1964. The Fine Arts, in: PLUMB, J. (ed) *Crisis in the Humanities*. Harmondsworth, Penguin; p. 121.
27 See Chapter 11.
28 KLEINBAUER, E. 1971. *Modern Perspectives in Western Art History*. Holt Rinehart Winston; pp. 1–35.

29 HADJINICOLAOU, *ibid*. Note 1.
30 RUIZ DE LA MATA, E. 1973. The Art Critic as Pedagogue, in: BATTCOCK, *ibid*. Note 3; p. 142.
31 FULLER, P. 1985. Rocks and Flesh; introduction to catalogue, Norwich School of Art Gallery.
32 SLOAN; in BATTCOCK, *ibid*. Note 3.
33 ACTON; *ibid*. Note 9.

Chapter Thirteen

ROSALIND BILLINGHAM Art History and Art Students

> Art history is still introduced into college curricula as a way of
> satisfying the authorities that students are capable of thinking as
> well as working with their hands [1].

In this sentence, Marcia Pointon (1980) identified the greatest problem
of teaching art history to practitioners today; too often patronising attitudes have left a legacy of resentment and prejudice against the subject
which obscures its true worth.

In the Autumn of 1963, art history was introduced as a compulsory
subject in British art colleges for the first time. This was one result of
the setting up of the National Committee for Diplomas in Art and
Design in May 1961, and was part of a process, which continued over
the next few years, of shifting mainstream art instruction from further
to higher education. The possibilities of better funding and enhanced
prestige were powerful motivating forces for a number of academic
decisions taken at that time, but compulsory art history can now be
viewed against wider tendencies in the art world. During the 1960s in
the heyday of Greenberg, formalism, and the Pop artists, reactions
against historical traditions were fierce. It was, perhaps, an instinctive
fear of art education being cut off from the historical roots which
nourished it, that led administrations in search of academic respectability
to alight on art history as a key subject, rather than English literature,
or the acquisition of a foreign language.

It is the contention of this chapter that art historians have a valuable
part to play in students' artistic development, provided that they recognise that different approaches are often required from those that are
generally approved in other areas of teaching. Janet Wolff (1981) has
referred to 'the conception of the artist as unique and gifted individual',
and has pointed out that this idea belongs to a particular historical situation [2]. The concept may be challenged, but contemporary British art
education is certainly linked to that notion; emphasis is less on a body
of knowledge common to all students, than on originality and indi-
viduality. These words are hard to define, but in practice seem to cause
more difficulty to theorists, than to artists and their tutors who usually
recognise these qualities instinctively when they see them.

In contra-distinction to students in most other areas of higher
education, artists are mainly taught as individuals rather than in classes,
and if art history is not to remain an uncomfortable excrescence of the
body of their course and is to fulfil any positive role in their creative
development, this fact must be faced. The stimulus of individual interests is often the first priority for student practitioners; on the other

hand another reason for teaching art history is that a more comprehensive approach opens up a wider range of traditions with which students can identify their positions. A common solution to these aspects of teaching has been to offer a wide range of options for study, where lectures are offered to small groups, and work expected from students agreed on an individual basis.

As Marcia Pointon (1980) has written, 'some would argue that students have to discover unaided what might contribute to their creative effort' [3]. Such an attitude, if carried to an extreme, could not only undermine the notion that art history can stimulate creativity, but also question the validity of much more art school teaching generally considered useful.

Itten (1961) in his attitude to the teaching of colour provides us with a sensible approach which can be applied to art history for the practitioner. His answer to questions about the reason for studying colour theory was:

> If you unknowing, are able to create masterpieces in color, then unknowledge is your way. But if you are unable to create masterpieces in color out of your un-knowledge then you ought to look for knowledge.

He continued:

> Doctrines are best for weaker moments. In moments of strength, problems are solved intuitively, as if of themselves [4].

It is arguable that the study of art history is not primarily for artists' moments of strength but for times of weakness which everyone experiences. As it embraces so much more than colour theory, it should, at some time provide succour for all. Artists who have very few moments of weakness are hardly likely to be full-time students.

A real difficulty, which has increased in recent years with the rapid expansion of the subject, lies in deciding what it actually embraces. Ernst Gombrich (1973), offered a common sense view of the problem in his Romanes lecture when he stated 'We cannot and need not put any theoretical limits to the historian's curiosity' [5]. We might add 'or the students'. Gombrich proceeded to demonstrate how economic, sociological, and technical studies all provided insight into the way in which the Sheldonian theatre came into being. To some extent the subject under consideration will suggest the approach; a full understanding of *Guernica*, for example, clearly demands some knowledge of Spanish political history.

The relationship of the teaching of art history, to the establishment and maintenance of standards grows increasingly complex, but it is still possible to argue that there can be an important and positive link. For many, it is now hard to accept the notion of one canon of indisputable masters whose excellence should be an example to others. Such an attitude was common in the nineteenth century, but Paul Hetherington (1978) who has made a study of the accepted major artists whose images appeared on a selection of buildings in Europe and America between 1777 and 1909, shows that even in the nineteenth century there were wide differences of opinion [6]. In a decade such as ours which has been

150

characterised by the plurality of approaches to contemporary art, divergent attitudes are inevitable. This does not necessarily invalidate the notion of canons in art, but, in the late twentieth century alternatives must be recognised. There is not only the mainstream, of Cézanne, Matisse and Picasso, but, for example, the cult of the naïve, which elevates Le Douanier Rousseau, Grandma Moses and Alfred Wallis. Paradoxically, and most importantly, one might construct a canon of significant rebels who have rejected dominant value systems, from Courbet, via Marinetti, to Duchamp, Rauschenberg and Johns.

In practice, many day-to-day attempts to engage young artists' interest could be described as relating their work to a suitable tradition with its corresponding canon. The chief difficulty is that saints are not normally canonised in their life-time; that is usually the privilege of a younger generation. By trying to make some sense of the recent past, we may enable young practitioners to see who is significant and creative; if, however, we are too dogmatic we may obscure new developments. What is quite certain is that it is very difficult for them to recognise originality from a position of ignorance.

Recently it has become fashionable to make comparisons with the structure of language. One fundamental truth can be stated in respect of this; if a language were to be wholly original, it would be totally incomprehensible. This is surely one of the most potent arguments for teaching students sufficient art history for them to know which tradition they wish to adopt and develop. As David Hockney (1976) remarked: 'People are not looking at the past sufficiently hard to see that within it there is some coherence and it can be sorted out' [7].

Art history can be specially valuable for those who feel inhibited by the personal nature of their own ideas. Private fantasies are an important artistic source, but, as Freud observed, an artist has the capacity to work over his day-dreams and make them lose what is too personal. He thus makes it possible for others to share in their enjoyment [8]. Students trying to develop this ability need to realise that, if they look hard enough and long enough, they will find some visual expression of their dream world on which they can build so that it no longer seems peculiarly strange to others.

Proficiency in art history frequently complements excellence in the studio, but we should, on the other hand, remember T. S. Eliot's remark that the person who contributes to culture, is not always a 'cultured person' [9]. So long as art training in this country remains within the framework of academic institutions, it may not be expedient to recognise this paradox, but art historians must not assume without question that there is an automatic equation between knowledge of their subject, and the fertilisation of creative thought.

Part of the challenge of Eliot's remark lies in how we interpret the vexed word 'culture'. Art history has traditionally been concerned with 'high culture', a term often associated with the highest endeavours of the human mind and spirit, rather than including 'all the characteristic activities and interests of a people' [10]. This attitude is well expressed by Gombrich when he speaks of 'that dreadful fall-out of the tourist industry, the horrors we see in the souvenir shops all over the world, which really do not belong to the history of art' [11]. Perhaps not, but the way visual trash has been used by artists is certainly important. Claes Oldenburg (1961) came near to describing Gombrich's horrors: 'I am for the art of cheap plaster and enamel' [12], and David Smith commented: 'It always surprises me, but where art comes from is spiritually much closer to the dump and discard of the culture' [13]. The perfection of Raphael offers little possibility for further development, but for Oldenburg (1961) 'scratchings in the asphalt, daubings on the walls', have indicated new directions [14]. Dubuffet and Art Brut showed us this particularly clearly. If art history is to stimulate creativity, none of 'the characteristic activities and interests of a people' can necessarily be ignored.

A liberal attitude towards what may constitute a suitable subject for visual education is prevalent in many art faculties, but artists today are faced with a bewildering variety of choices made even greater by improved communications. Art historians can at least suggest some routes through the maze, provided they remember that many people will find the visual experiences of everyday life particularly interesting, with all their variety and crudity.

The teaching of art history to art students has not, on the whole, been sufficiently studied either by practitioners or by the art historians themselves. Clearly, priorities and emphases are not necessarily the same as when teaching non-executant groups. In the latter case, teaching students to look may be more evenly balanced with historical, philosophical and social considerations concerned with relating art history to the wider history of ideas. With artists it is often practical to be highly selective in the presentation of historical data in the interests of more purely visual education. John A. Walker (1980) has published his views on this issue from experience gained at Middlesex Polytechnic. He developed a seminar course on what he called 'pictorial rhetoric' or 'how pictures work, how they communicate meaning' [15]. He confessed that he had discussed at least one image 'in a situation which necessarily severed the picture from its social and historical context' and continued:

> Another art historian might argue that it is precisely that context
> which I should have provided . . . However, given the objectives of
> the course—to teach students the rudiments of pictorial rhetoric so
> that they can articulate statements about the world in which they
> live—some violence to the past, was, in my view, justified [16].

We may not fully understand how a work communicates meaning without some knowledge of its historical background, iconography, and contemporary interpretation. But, as Philip Rawson (1969), pointed out when discussing the appreciation of drawing 'The forms . . . and the principles they follow are the key to what the draughtsman meant to say about his topic, and reveal his mind.' [17]

The balance between visual analysis and historical, economic and social considerations must depend on how tutor and students see the role of art in human affairs. The 1981 debate at the University of British Columbia between Clement Greenberg and Timothy Clark, excellently summarised by Paul Richter (1982) in *Art Monthly*, was widely followed because two dominant positions were clearly articulated [18]. Greenberg, as a critic, holds the view that quality is the most important aspect of any work of art, and that what underlies quality may be found in the works of art themselves. Clark, as an historian, while not indifferent to quality, particularly values art that is responsive to the social order in which it occurs. For him, the historical background is vital to understanding. While few practitioners would concern themselves with the details of this debate, a number are aware of the increasing trend towards the political and social interpretation of works of art for which historical knowledge is necessary.

The most obvious use of art history to contemporary artists is to illuminate the present. This is the students' starting point, and quite frequently, the place at which we have to begin. Few historians study periods which are entirely irrelevant to current concerns, but the artist may be much more interested in tracing links backwards rather than forwards. Contemporary American Realism may lead to a study of Courbet, or Imaged Expressionism to Kirchner more easily than a strictly chronological approach would do.

Such differences of approach do not in themselves constitute sufficient reason for believing that the teaching of art history to art students is a specific vocation. But understanding some inner resistances to the subject is essential for success, and discussion of them important. As Hockney (1976) put it 'The reason for not looking at art from other periods is based on a fear of something . . . anybody who's gone through the thing of becoming an artist knows about it' [19]. The vital question is whether all art historians know about it, or, if they do, treat artists accordingly. Common humanity usually suggests that we do not deliberately expose people to that which frightens them; rather we try to dispose of the fear. It is frequently concerned with loss of artistic identity, or sometimes with the seeming impossibility of being able to produce images comparable in quality with those of the past. Originality within identifiable traditions needs to be discussed and students helped to gain confidence gradually. Another fear encountered is that of a loss of visual innocence. It needs to be pointed out that we are all bombarded by potent and persuasive images from the mass media, and that we do not ignore them. It is impossible to maintain the innocence of a child in this, as in other aspects of life.

The most obvious objection to art history is that its study takes people away from the studio too long and too often. A clear remedy is to find effective ways for the historian to work in the studio, to attend discussions and to contribute to assessments. Common ground can be found in a study of techniques; as Waldemar Januszczak (1980) has pointed out, such an approach is a realistic and fascinating guide to the development of Western art [20].

One potential benefit of compulsory art history since the 1960s is that recent generations of studio tutors know something about it. However, they are sometimes the people who have experienced, and found obnoxious, the attitude that the study of art, unsupported by history or theory, is not itself a sufficiently intellectual challenge for the award of a degree. The case for art history cannot be based on intellectual stiffening; in any case a wide range of academic disciplines would be equally valuable in this respect. It must, instead, be based on an awareness of its importance to the creative development of the young artist and to the understanding of the world he or she inhabits.

When it demonstrates such significance, young artists need little persuasion to look at the art of the past of their own volition. Indeed, some of their recent heroes have demanded a knowledge of art history. One cannot fully understand Anselm Kiefer without a knowledge of Friedrich, or Julian Schnabel without a passing acquaintance with Gaudi's mosaics—while Peter Blake's *The Meeting, or Have a Nice Day Mr Hockney* becomes meaningless without knowing Courbet's precedent. The *Twentieth Century German Art* exhibition focused our attention on

47   GUSTAVE COURBERT *The Meeting, or Bonjour M. Courbet*, 1854, oil on canvas 47·25 × 58·75"; Musée Fabre, Montpelier. (photo: Bridgeman Art Library)

48   PETER BLAKE *The Meeting, or Have a Nice Day Mr Hockney*, 1981–5, oil on
canvas 38·5 × 48.75″; Tate Gallery, London, reproduced courtesy of the artist.

the use and re-use of traditional iconography to give it contemporary
relevance [21]. The peculiarly-German problem of artists born after 1945,
confronting their artistic heritage without incurring political misinter-
pretation, provided a centre of interest for all those struggling to make
their art comprehensible by relating it to various forms of traditional
iconography, as well for as those involved with the increasing politicis-
ation of art.

   While these considerations seem to have made art history still more
important for artists, other developments typified by the work of
Stephen Willats have complicated a number of issues. Believing that art
has become more and more distant from the main body of society, he
has been concerned to communicate with a section of the populace who
would never normally enter a gallery. Working on West London housing
estates, Willats has adopted techniques more familiar to the behavioural
sciences than to art, in order to find out about the inhabitants and their
homes, occupations and aspirations. This has become the central subject-
matter of his work, such as the *Tower Block* drawings of March 1984.

Such work owes little to traditional artistic practice or its history, but it does appear to interest the people on the estates. This aspect of artistic practice cannot be ignored. It is presented as photographic collage and montage, often with hand-written captions and commentary. It raises questions not only about the nature of art and its purpose, but also about the phenomena that must now be accepted into art history.

The chief challenge to traditional forms in the visual arts, and to supporting studies including art history, must surely be television and the associated areas which have developed in polytechnics in recent years, under umbrella titles such as 'Media and Cultural Studies'. Often these areas have been popular with students as a way of coming to terms with the society in which they live. Intellectual developments and the possibilities of the new media call for particular clarity of thought on the part of artists, and a knowledge of historical precedent is useful to put problems in perspective. The development of oil painting in fifteenth century Flanders did not immediately alter the style or subject-matter of the miniaturists who had painted manuscripts, though it gradually extended their range and their public. By the same token, computers do not necessarily alter the central concerns of those who use them. As a BBC television series recently showed, Howard Hodgkin could still work on *commedia dell'arte* themes for Pulcinella by computer with a Quantel 'paintbox', and Sidney Nolan has worked in a similar way on his *Ned Kelly* themes [22].

History also shows that new statements and fresh visual languages can be made with traditional media. Cubism was developed in oil paint, but became the language of *Guernica*, arguably the greatest political painting of the twentieth century. On the other hand, few would deny that new media may trigger important artistic developments. Video and computer graphics have clearly opened up new possibilities, though these have sometimes been exploited best by people professionally involved in graphics and television, rather than by those traditionally considered to be artists.

Questioning the institutional definitions of art and art history has long been a preoccupation of Marxist art historians on the one hand, and of artists as various as Duchamp, Johns and Willats on the other. Fresh challenges will doubtless arise from those who work in an ever widening variety of new media. Just as film studies are a generally accepted part of art school curricula, masters of the video camera and the computer may well be the subjects of historical study in the twenty-first century. But a wide range of symbolic forms and stylistic languages will still be significant, and for this reason art history's curricular importance is unlikely to decline.

Notes and References

1 POINTON, M. 1980 *History of Art: A Students Handbook*, p. ix. London, Allen & Unwin.
2 WOLFF, J. 1981 *The Social Production of Art*, p. 27. London, Macmillan.
3 POINTON, M., *op. cit.*, p. 12.

4 ITTEN, J. 1961 *The Art of Color*, p. 12. New York, Reinhold.
5 GOMBRICH, E. 1973 Art History and the Social Sciences, reprinted in *Ideals and Idols*, p. 133. Oxford, Phaidon.
6 HETHERINGTON, P. 1978 Pantheons in the *Mouseion*. *Art History* I, No. 2, pp. 214–228.
7 HOCKNEY, D. 1976 *David Hockney*, p. 130. London, Thames and Hudson.
8 FREUD, S. 1916–17 (translated by STRACHEY, J.) *Introductory Lectures on Psychoanalysis*, Standard Edition, Vol. XVI, p. 374. London, Hogarth Press.
9 ELIOT, T. S. 1962 *Notes Towards the Definition of Culture*, 2nd edition, p. 23. London, Faber.
10 ELIOT, T. S. 1962 *ibid.* p. 31.
11 GOMBRICH, E. 1973 *op. cit.*, p. 151.
12 OLDENBURG, C. 1961 Statement for 'Environments Situations Spaces' at the Martha Jackson Gallery New York, 1961. in *Store Days*, 1967, p. 40. New York, Something Else Press.
13 SMITH, D. 1968 *David Smith, Sculpture and Writings*, p. 77. London, Thames and Hudson.
14 OLDENBURG, C. 1961 *op. cit.*, p. 40.
15 WALKER, J. 1980 Teaching Art History, *Block* No. 1, p. 2.
16 WALKER, J. 1980 *ibid.*, p. 4.
17 RAWSON, P. 1969 *Drawing*, p. 5. London, Oxford University Press.
18 RICHTER, P. 1982 Modernism and After, Part I. *Art Monthly*, No. 54 March 1982, pp. 3–7; Part II, No. 55 April 1982, pp. 5–8.
19 HOCKNEY, D. 1976 *op. cit.*, p. 87.
20 JANUSZCZAK, W. (ed.) 1980 *Techniques of the World's Great Painters*, p. 7. Oxford, Phaidon.
21 ROYAL ACADEMY OF ARTS. 1985. *German Art in the C20th: Painting and Sculpture 1905–1985*. London.
22 *Painting with Light: Howard Hodgkin*. BBC2 20 May 1987.
    Painting with Light: Sidney Nolan. BBC2 27 May 1987.

Chapter Fourteen

JOHN SWIFT The Use of Art and Design Education Archives in Critical Studies

The literature of *Critical Studies* has emphasised a need for balance in the art and design curriculum—a balance that couples practical artistry with, among other things, critical, historical, cultural and aesthetic activities. Art and design education research over the past twenty years has pointed to the predominance of practice, and to the scant attention paid to parallel development of articulate verbal reaction, reflection, analysis, and synthesis. The impact of this partial neglect of the learners' abilities to demonstrate informed views of their own work, and that of their peers, is considerable, as is also the general lack of learner inter-action with work of other periods, cultures, and the contemporary public art world. The historical reasons for this imbalance have been argued with varying success, and suggestions made concerning necessary correc-tive actions for art and design teachers, art advisers, art galleries and museums, artist placements, and the disciplines of art and design history.

Rather than add to these positions, I wish to explore here a related but different use of resources: the use of art and design education archives. Thus this chapter will explore: (a) the currently typical use of historical and contemporary collections of art, in order to develop (b) a distinctive method, unique to art and design education archives, that places initial attention on the teacher rather than the pupil. What I am proposing is in effect a form of critical study that affects learning by initially informing teaching. In so doing I hope to suggest the potential validity of retrieving and re-studying past teaching practices, which only too often are erroneously considered moribund.

Much *Critical Studies* literature has been concerned with the relative merits of exposing children and students to first-hand experience of artefacts in galleries and museums, the preparation towards such ex-perience through books, slides, films and videos in the classroom, and the ways in which such developing awareness can be harnessed to the learners' growing repertoires of skills, knowledge and aesthetic capabilities.

In art galleries and museums, the artefacts on display are invariably the works of artists, craftspersons, or more rarely designers, of estab-lished reputations. The artefacts act as exemplars of particular approaches, methods, or theories within specific social and cultural contexts. A variety of models of enquiry for pupils are generally possible, some of which derive from art and design history, others from social history, psychology or philosophy. While the latter have been used sporadically, the former have gained a strong position. But what kind of position has been advocated? A traditional approach has derived from iconography: used by itself, this has been called into question from many quarters. And a related approach, chronologically ordering and linearly defining bodies of knowledge, has often led to a sort of historical determinism.

The use of either method in schools too frequently leads to Eurocentric conceptions of art, and a sense of art and its history being separate from the learners' experience. However, an argument over more appropriate methods within art history is not the central issue here. The point I wish to make is that, whether the learner is being put into contact with a sketch, a maquette, a preparatory drawing or a finished work, the status of the artefact has already been determined *by its selection*. It is 'real' art, craft or design, and it is an object: it is process reified. These remarks are not to deny the value of such study, but merely to indicate a possible tendency towards the stereotypical.

It is the educational purpose of such study I wish to examine. For anything long-lastingly useful and fundamental to arise from an acquaintance with artefacts, the learners have to be able to relate the experience to their own knowledge, and intelligently and sensitively assimilate it to practice. This means understanding something of the artistic *process* in making an artefact, and by this I do not mean merely the assimilation of technical style and skill. Unless the sense of procedural discovery within the artist's work (the enquiry, hypothesis, alternating ideas, uncertainty, and resolution) is translated into the learner's consciousness, then only partially reusable learning will have ensued. The learners should be helped, through the study of artefacts and/or artists, to assimilate and develop similarly self-referential and questioning stances.

Such conscious awareness of the pupils' own learning procedures could also be applied to the procedures by which they are educated—that is, those of their teachers. What I am referring to is a self-conscious awareness of learning processes—a sense of identification, on the part of the pupil, with the rationale, method or model of teaching being employed, whether it is teacher-, learner-, or discipline-centred. Although this *may* be achieved by the study of artefacts and statements of established artists and designers, it can be accomplished more directly through the use of art and design education archives.

These generally differ from the usual collections of art galleries and museums, in that their evidence is primarily concerned with ways of teaching and their outcomes. I do not wish to draw too fine a distinction here, because what is in evidence in art galleries and museums frequently reveals learning strategies too. However, these are usually part of a mature process of learning, and it is questionable whether young children should be asked to ape the work of adults. The significance of our small number of art and design education archives is that much of the work held is invariably the result of some form of *institutional* art, craft or design education, and as such—by revealing intention, method and result—has potential relevance for current teachers. Thus I am switching attention away from the pupil and directing it towards the teacher; for if learners are to have conscious knowledge of the teaching that they undergo, it follows that teachers themselves must have clearer, articulated conceptual bases for their practice. One way of ensuring that this is brought sharply to teachers' attention is by the study of different models of art, craft and design education. The importance of art and design education archives is in their potential to reveal such models.

There are two reasons why I have drawn attention to the teacher. One is logistical: the small number and limited resources of most of our archives prevent large-scale visiting by pupils, although touring exhibitions offer a partial solution. The other is educational: to change learners' awareness on a broad scale requires first an alteration, modification or enhancement of teacher awareness.

It is a common claim among art, craft and design teachers that they lack the time and opportunity to visit and study alternative teaching styles in other schools, and have few occasions for disinterested discussion of rationales for their subject. Much of any discussion that does take place is related to the perceived needs of examinations, and may only touch on current and short-term issues of concern. The opportunity to study alternative systems and styles for their own sake, as well as for their applicability, may be provided through the use of art and design education archives. Before developing a proposal that has derived from experiments in use, I should first of all describe art and design education archives, for they are a relatively new phenomenon and are perhaps not widely known.

The idea of gathering together children's art work to form a national collection has arisen with some urgency from time to time over the past fifty years. Good intentions were often unrealised due to lack of finance, grandiose planning, and geographic rivalry. Collections were made privately but not publicly identified, and access was therefore limited if not impossible. Thus from 1985 a group of individuals representing privately-held or institutionally-owned collections met to try to create some form of network of association. By limiting aims and scope, the group was able to form the *National Association of Art and Design Education Archives* in 1986. Current associates are Birmingham Polytechnic, Bretton Hall, London University Institute of Education, the Victoria and Albert Museum (Art and Design Archive), and Wiltshire Museum and Library Service.

Whilst the different associates have common aims to preserve, enhance awareness of, and draw attention to the need to collect and keep old and current information, they retain independent collecting, indexing, financing, advertising and planning policies. Thus the V&A Archive has an extremely broad range of artefacts and documentation, much of which would come under the gallery and museum definition offered above. Bretton Hall has a collecting and purchasing policy, and has built up a wide and varied range of material in part due to the generosity of a local patron. Its collection is directly art educational, and contains, for example, Don Pavey's *Colour* collection, written material by a number of art, craft and design educators, collections of visual and written material associated with Alexander Barclay-Russell, Franz Cizek, and

160

Albert Halliwell, as well as examples of group approaches, such as the *Basic Design* movement. At the time of writing, Bretton Hall has about thirty discrete representative topics in its collection, and there are plans to build an Archives Centre which will improve future use by both teachers and learners. Wiltshire Museum and Library Service has two main collections—one being a further Barclay-Russell archive, the other having been donated by Robin Tanner. London University Institute of Education has a large multi-national collection of student dissertations and papers deposited by former members of staff. The Department of Art at Birmingham Polytechnic has two main collections: papers and artefacts documenting the history of its art school from 1820 onwards; and the Marion Richardson Archive donated by her family. It also possesses smaller collections of visual work from Stourbridge Art School (*c* 1940–60) and some local schools.

The V&A and Wiltshire collections are held by institutions committed to making their holdings accessible. The others are held by educational institutions which, while restricting access to some degree, have greater potential to use their material for scholarly research and curriculum development. Nevertheless, until Bretton Hall has its new building in Autumn 1989, large-group access to any of the Association's collections will be problematic. In any case, for London and Birmingham, with no such accommodation plans, different means of dissemination will have to be developed. In the light of this necessity, then, it is the methods that have been used by Birmingham that I wish to explore at length.

Birmingham Polytechnic's policy has been to bring practising teachers into close contact with the theories and practice of Marion Richardson for the sake of their applicability to currect art education. This was done initially by proposing to the Department of Education and Science that Teacher Fellowships could be extended to art educational archive study. In 1984 with the co-operation of Manchester LEA, and the enthusiastic support of its Art Inspector Keith Gentle, a teacher was released to work partly in the archives and partly in five Manchester schools. This was funded by Manchester, and became a prototype for successive, DES-funded, Teacher Fellowships in Art Education, the first of their kind.

The Teacher Fellowships had to satisfy several parties. They had to be considered sufficiently relevant to persuade an Authority to release a teacher for a term; they had to have the potential to enrich a teacher's future practice; they had to spring from and therefore satisfy the individual teacher's interests; and they had to satisfy normal standards of academic research in the analytical reports that were lodged in the archive on completion. The sponsoring Authority retained all other work produced, and this was usually made available to other teachers by such means as slide-packs, illustrated talks and exhibitions. I hope to demonstrate the potential of this method by outlining the first three Teacher Fellowships undertaken, in order to reveal the impact on a teacher of studying a different teacher's ideas, methods and results.

The first Teacher Fellow was Eve Hart, a Manchester secondary school teacher. She had been attracted by the visual images produced by the teaching methods of Marion Richardson, but had subscribed to the commonly-held belief that the success of Richardson's work was due more to her unique personal abilities than the soundness of her educational aims. Hart had felt that it was probably Richardson's working relationships with pupils over many years that had led to the particular qualities that were observable in her pupils' work, and had enabled her to put so much trust in her pupils' own judgements. Hart was also intrigued by the idea of 'mind-picturing'—a Richardson method which allowed the pupil to let unconscious images float into the 'mind's eye'. Many results of this procedure are held in the archive, and most are non-figurative. She wondered whether in the present age of visual bombardment children would 'mind-picture' or visualise in the same way.

In order to test whether it was Richardson's familiarity with her pupils that had influenced the quality of her results, Hart deliberately chose to work in five different schools where she was unknown to the pupils. Richardson's charisma was more problematic, but Hart was to conclude that Richardson's success had in fact arisen more from drive and determination than charisma. She chose to use a particular order of experience for the pupils, beginning with 'mind-picturing', followed by 'word-picturing' (responding to verbal input with visual imagery), and 'beauty hunts' (visiting and discussing visual qualities of the school surrounds, and producing work from resulting memories).

49   M WAGSTAFF *Mind Picture*, undated, Dudley Girls' High School. Marion Richardson Archive, Cat. No. MRA 4921, City of Birmingham Polytechnic.

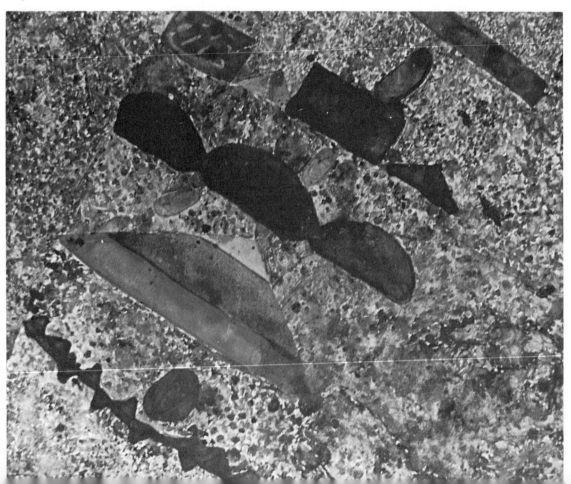

50 CHI WAY HO *Mind Picture*, (Krystyn Cieslik, Teacher Fellow), Manchester, 1985, Department of Education and Science/City of Manchester Education Authority.

The secondary school children with whom Hart worked had been mostly educated through direct observational methods. Despite this, and the strangeness of her requests, they displayed surprising willingness and ability to 'see' mind-pictures that bore a strong family resemblance to those in the Richardson Archive. She chose similarly-worded descriptions to those of Richardson's for her word-pictures, and again was surprised how much the children could retain in their minds' eyes. Similar findings were obtained for the beauty hunts also. She became increasingly aware of the ability of children both to allow mental images to form, and, on prompting, to form images of surprising complexity. She also realised that the children's typical use of colour and pigment was unable to cope with the mental images, and that experimental work was necessary to assist this—a provision Richardson had built into her teaching.

The next, DES-funded, teacher was also from Manchester. Krystyn Cieslik had heard of Hart's research and become interested partly because, while she had little formal knowledge of Richardson's teaching methods, her own were to some degree similar, and partly because of the reputed beneficial effects of Richardson's methods on children's behaviour. Many of Cieslik's own pupils had special needs or learning difficulties caused by social, maturational, behavioural or linguistic problems. She wanted to test whether Richardson's mind-picturing and word-picturing ideas would work with children who normally had very small concentration spans, were predisposed to be unruly, and had very low senses of self-expectation and esteem. Verbal communication was a further problem, and she wished to improve this by using the Richardson method of having children evaluate the success of their pictures in relation to their mental images.

51 ANON. *Word Picture:*
Moonlit Night, undated,
Dudley Girls' High
School. Marion
Richardson Archive, Cat.
No. MRA NC, City of
Birmingham Polytechnic.

52 SHAGUFTA *Word*
Picture: Moonlit Night,
(Krystyn Cieslik, Teacher
Fellow), Manchester, 1985,
Department of Education
and Science/City of Man-
chester Education Authority.

53   A WOOD *Beauty Hunt: Untitled*, undated, Dudley Girls' High School. Marion Richardson Archive, Cat. No. MRA 7086, City of Birmingham Polytechnic.

54   RIZWANA *Beauty Hunt: the Pot Shop*, (Krystyn Cieslik, Teacher Fellow), Manchester, 1985, Department of Education and Science/City of Manchester Education Authority.

55   R HAMILTON (9 years)
Handwriting Pattern,
undated. Marion
Richardson Archive, Cat.
No. MRA 8000, City of
Birmingham Polytechnic.

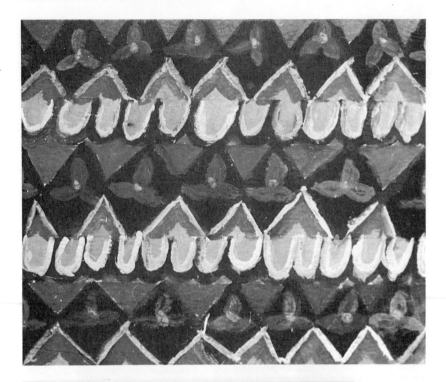

56   ZOE (11 years)
Handwriting Pattern, (Eve
Hart, Teacher Fellow),
Manchester, 1984,
Department of
Education and Science/
City of Manchester
Education Authority.

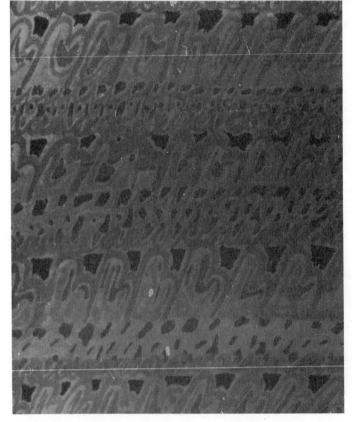

She found a remarkable change of interest level and skill arising from the mind-picture. She had stressed that each individual's imagery would be different (following Richardson's beliefs) and that the results of their mental images, if honestly transcribed, would be unique. The children relished the idea of uniqueness, and this seemed to have a beneficial effect on their motivation. The word-pictures, too, were far more successful than Cieslik had anticipated. The qualities of colour, tonal variation, and texture were in advance of anything produced previously. Not only was motivation to produce artefacts noticeably increased, but the children's willingness to discuss their own and others' pictures increased also. Cieslik noticed a more rapid assimilation and remembering of art terms, and improvement in general behaviour and attitude. Absenteeism and lateness were much reduced, while voluntary quietness, attention, concentration and confident use of language all increased.

Cieslik concluded that the emphasis on personal discovery, self-evaluation and individual 'uniqueness' had beneficially altered her pupils' self-esteem, and that this had led to greater confidence, attention and concentration, which in turn had led to skilled art work, extended vocabulary and improved behaviour. She was aware that this could have been due to the Hawthorne effect (ie, that it was the extra attention that the pupils received, rather than any precise teaching input, that had altered their responses), but felt that the correlation between her aims and the results were too specific for this to have been the case.

The third Teacher Fellow was also from Manchester. Barbara Kinch worked in primary education and was intrigued by the possibility of transferring Richardson's methods to this level. She was aware of some of the handwriting and pattern-making that Richardson had advocated, but wished to explore children's capacities to use mind-pictures, word-pictures and beauty hunts. Kinch wished to explore what further learning would be generated by these methods (for example, colour mixing, media experiment, or colour memory) and decided to create a visual environment consistent with Richardson's beliefs and practice.

She surrounded the children with objects, pictures and artefacts with particular attention to their colour. She arranged and numbered over a hundred skeins of wool, grouped according to colour to form a central feature in the art room, with duplicate unnumbered skeins placed in a different part of the room. This was used to encourage colour matching by memory. Coloured paints were displayed in transparent jars; coloured liquids were similarly housed against the windows, along with overlapping coloured tissues. A display of fabrics, weavings, plants and stones was chosen for its evidence of colour contrast and harmony. Reproductions of art were carefully interspersed with these objects to reveal different types of usage of the adjacent, displayed colours. The interest this generated enabled her to have a constantly changing display as children, parents and other teachers brought further wools, objects and transparent containers. Within this visually stimulating environment Kinch explored the mind-picture, word-picture and beauty hunt.

She found that the children's willingness to both produce mind-pictures and talk about them exceeded her expectations. Colour experiments were quickly assimilated to mind-pictures, and open discussion and co-operation were strongly evident. Word-pictures (using Richardson's descriptions) produced considerable thought about medium, tone, and richness of colour. The children often persisted for two afternoons on the same picture in order that their paintings would match the richness of their mental images. Kinch used the beauty hunt also, finding the children's memory of objects and colours enhanced by the planned interjection of colour-matching exercises and colour memory lessons. The children's vocabulary developed in accordance with their more heightened awareness of colour and their ability to mix complicated colours.

Kinch concluded that any reservations she may have had over the appropriateness of Richardson's methods for primary school children were mistaken. She was conscious of allowing the children more re-sponsibility in evaluating their own work, and of the resultant positive responses. She became progressively aware that the child's capacity for visual memory was an untapped source in most primary education. Teachers accepted it, but rarely built on it. She also became aware of having to prevent herself offering solutions on request, in that the Richardson method always re-addressed the request to the questioner. She found herself more and more in agreement with Richardson's belief that the children's work should be assessed in the light of richer or poorer responses, rather than correct or incorrect.

These particular examples of three Teacher Fellows, working on similar lines based on another teacher's ideas and methods (in this case from an earlier period) not only materially affected the ways the children in their care worked, but—arguably more importantly—affected the thinking and beliefs of the teachers themselves. The potential long-term effects of these changes are important. They manifest themselves in five different ways:

Educational planning

While all conscientious teachers plan and prepare their lessons, the conscious awareness of planning for the unexpected (ie. using another teacher's methods) draws extra attention to order, contents, materials, and their interaction.

Lesson content

The Teacher Fellows were faced with the alternative of using Richardson's own contents and/or adapting them. For example, in the use of the word-picture they could have used her verbal descriptions literally, or by bringing them up to date in terms of detail, or, through an analysis of her descriptive method, formulating new descriptions. The mind-picture was resistant to modification by its nature, and the beauty hunt obviously depended upon the actual environment used. The need to extemporise concerning colour and media experiments was quickly learned, and rapidly incorporated into the overall plans of the Teacher

Fellows' lessons. The greater emphasis on the children's verbal reactions, externalisation of ideas, and emerging evaluative powers, also had implications for the content of lessons.

The art work

Each Teacher Fellow was aware that she was in some way challenging the orthodoxies of art lessons by her activities. The emphasis on personally-generated images, the need to find techniques to correspond with the visual qualities of mental images, the impact of a richer, directed visual environment, led to children's work which the Teacher Fellows believed could not have been achieved by other means. Results often exceeded their expectations for particular groups of children and for many individuals. The art work looked different—it had a different flavour from that produced by direct observation alone, surpassing it in terms of colour, tonal variety, and the technical means of experimental expression, as well as in personal identity. It alerted attention to the possibility that an exclusive diet of observational study might be seriously neglecting vital aspects of art-making.

Children's learning

The emphasis on self-evaluation in discussion and in the writing of comments on the pictures (especially the mind-pictures) became increasingly important. The children's growing ability to make judgements was linked with their developing awareness of the uniqueness of their imagery. Their ability to make the painted images correspond with their mental images was also growing through experimental colour and media exercises. This confidence was reflected in an increase of vocabulary skills, media manipulation, self-dependency, group cohesiveness, concentration span, and, in one study, improvement of overall behaviour.

Teaching style

The methods used called into question each Teacher Fellow's teaching habits. Each became increasingly aware of her tendency to offer prompt answers to questions, and that this effectively reduced further questions, and probably led to children too readily doubting their own abilities to provide answers. Readdressing questions to the questioners in an intelligent and sympathetic manner began to convince the children that they had inherent capacities to discover answers for themselves. A shift in the Teacher Fellows' thinking was taking place where they were questioning their roles as purveyors of knowledge, and trying different roles—those of facilitator and mediator.

Contrary to the mythologies surrounding Richardson's teaching (particularly those of 'free expression' and 'non-intervention') the Teacher Fellows found that their methods called for considerable organisational powers, pre-planning, environmental organisation, conscious suspension of value judgements, and labour-intensive, sensitive responses to each and every individual. The teacher's role was significant rather than marginal.

According to eye-witnesses, Richardson's lessons were orderly, quiet, and even contemplative. The methods of mind-picturing seem to assist this: to succeed, the children have to be engrossed in their work, self-dependent, mutually-supportive, and self-evaluating. In fact evaluation involved a major shift for all the Teacher Fellows. Normally they would have awarded marks or some other notation without any thought of detailed consultation with the maker. Richardson's methods did not allow this. Instead the children had to evaluate their own works in relation to their mental images. The classes also had a role in evaluating the successful and less successful pictures, and this they did with considerable skill and sensitivity. The teacher's evaluatory role was generally not to comment in terms of correctness or incorrectness, but to judge how well and fully the picture had developed from the mental image that the child had verbally articulated, and to do this in consultation with the whole class. This method offered each Teacher Fellow comparisons with her usual practice, enabling her to consider the significance of criteria that are developed from individual pieces of work, as opposed to those that are determined in advance of any specific work.

In conclusion: the importance of this research method is not in the fact that three teachers learned how Marion Richardson worked over sixty years ago, although this historical aspect is valuable, but that they studied and implemented an alternative teaching philosophy by immersing themselves in it. By so doing they were brought face-to-face with their usual practices, and by meeting them consciously had to reconsider their beliefs and teaching styles. They became more critically aware of some of their unspoken beliefs and practices, and of the limitations of some orthodoxies that currently exist in art education.

I am not suggesting that this model of enquiry is the only possible one for art and design education archives. The study of artefacts by pupils (given that direct access to them is possible); the application of research to educational theory through the study of written and wrought materials; historical research for its own sake—these more customary methods are of course valuable. But the point is that in art and design education archives we have the *unique* opportunity to examine and understand different systems of art teaching, and by using archival holdings as applied models, allow teachers to focus and reconsider their philosophy, beliefs and methods in the light of challenging alternatives. The vital feature of this approach is that teachers become more aware of their own learning capacities when challenged by the unexpected or the different. This is commonly expected of the learners within our care. Such experiences of process-oriented study may therefore have nothing but benefit for the teacher's ability to assist learning. By undertaking their own form of *Critical Study* and questioning customary aims, content, beliefs, reference sources, teaching style, evaluation and outcomes, teachers will be better able to decide upon and implement learning activities within the range of practical, expressive, aesthetic, cultural, historical and critical alternatives.

Index